LEARN TO DRIVE

IN
PICTURES

by

A. Tom Topper

PAPERFRONTS
ELLIOT RIGHT WAY BOOKS
KINGSWOOD, SURREY, U.K.

Typeset in 9½/10pt Times by County Typesetters,
Margate, Kent.

Made and Printed in Great Britain by Richard Clay Ltd.,
Bungay, Suffolk.

CONTENTS

PART THREE
JUNCTIONS

PART FOUR
BAD WEATHER – NIGHT DRIVING
AUTOMATICS – FRIGHTS – SKIDS
MOTORWAYS – QUESTIONS – YOUR TEST

GENERAL GUIDANCE

This book is planned to enable you to learn to drive starting from the first time you sit in a driving seat. My publishers guarantee that if you study it well you should pass your Test. If you fail, you can return the book for a full refund under their terms-of-sale on the back cover.

Your first task is to master control of the car. This *must* be complete *before* you head for the open road. In **PART ONE** I divide this *beginning* stage into three:

STAGE ONE is to familiarise yourself with the controls – not to try to drive.

STAGE TWO is OPEN SPACE PRACTICE. You need, with your teacher, to find a quiet open space and learn in safety to start smoothly, to stop (including being introduced to emergency stops), to steer, to change gear, to reverse and so on. Good places for this are worth seeking out; quiet empty car parks, disused air-strips, or dry fields (with farmer's permission) are examples. Failing these, choose a quiet area of side-roads as many driving schools do. You don't want hordes of other traffic making your job harder and you must avoid danger to children. Your teacher should drive there.

STAGE THREE is to learn proficiently to carry out the manoeuvring control tests expected on your Driving Test: the **Three-Point-Turn**, the **Reverse Into A Narrow Or Limited Opening** and the **Hill Start**. Your teacher should select suitable quiet locations for each of these. Again, he should always drive there.

Beginning with the above three stages in order *is the safest way to learn to drive*. Believe me, when you move on to **PART TWO**: GENERAL ROAD AND TRAFFIC DRIVING and then **PART THREE** and **PART FOUR**, the knowledge that you have already reached the Test standard in *car control* becomes very reassuring. It sets you free to concentrate on traffic, undistracted by worry about how to handle the car.

On the same score one of the first things you will do in

PART TWO is to look again at Emergency Stops. You will do some more, this time from faster speeds than before, to consolidate that work before driving on.

You have to have a current provisional driving licence. Application forms are obtained at most Post Offices (as are Test application forms). You cannot drive until you have received the licence, and you must have signed it in ink too! Study all the information sent to you with it. You must display standard-size **L** plates front and back (properly – not just stuck in the windows blocking your view). Your car must be taxed and insured. You have to have a qualified driver, aged 21 or over and who has held a licence for at least three years, to supervise and guide you.

It is essential that the insurance policy is endorsed if necessary to cover you as a Learner; it may cost a little extra but to drive without proper cover is illegal.

Apart from that legal point, you should also understand that your policy could become invalidated if you deliberately drive an unroadworthy vehicle, or if you are unfit through drink or drug etc. Alternatively, your insurance company may pay out for an accident and then sue you. Either way you could lose your all and be bankrupted – a horrifying prospect which could ruin your life for many years.

You *must* wear your glasses or contact lenses if you need them. (On Test the examiner will check whether you can read a car number plate a good 23 metres away.)

A GOOD TEACHER

Driving schools live by *local* reputation. In choosing a professional instructor it's best to seek out a named individual known to be good. Quite rightly, *any* experienced qualified driver (as above) may teach you, though none may charge who have not also passed the government instructors' test. Thus friends and relatives are also able to teach. Many of them with long accident-free mileages to their credit, do so supremely well. Indeed there is no evidence that the professionals achieve any better Test pass rate. For most Learners however, a combination of driving school lessons *and* practice with family or friends suits best. It makes gaining the necessary amount of experience behind the wheel for a pass, more affordable.

WHEN TO TAKE YOUR TEST

A Test failed, taken too early, is expensive and disappointing. My advice is wait until *you* begin to feel confident, and at the same time relaxed, at the wheel. When *you* feel you have got the measure of all that this book says, will be soon enough to book up your Test. Continuing with your practice whilst you are waiting should then give you the "edge" that will ensure a pass.

DO YOUR HOMEWORK

You must know the basic "rules of the road" from the Highway Code, in order to be safe at the wheel. So it *must* be studied *before* you go out for the first time. That learning will need to be reinforced as your lessons progress – to the degree that you become an "authority" on the Code generally, and on signs and road markings in particular, by the time of your Test.

You can improve your depth of knowledge of the Highway Code with companion *Paperfront* 'Highway Code Questions and Answers' by John Humphries. In **Q** and **A** format, this probes every aspect of the Code, and draws its answer to each question from all the sections of the Code which interrelate to that specific subject. It thus provides an unmatched learning formula.

You will be aware that by law you must wear your seat belt. You should remind other adults in the car though you cannot make them comply with the law. The safety of child passengers however, *is* the driver's responsibility whether or not a parent may say otherwise. You must absorb *in detail* the regulations set out in the Highway Code and keep abreast of any changes introduced from time to time. Did you know, for example, that children ought never to ride in the rear luggage compartment of an estate car except in purpose-built seats? Even in a minor shunt an unrestrained child cannot fail to be flung about – with potential for shocking damage to the head. Or, were you aware that in Court, after an accident, a driver or passenger not wearing a seat belt may be judged to blame for some of the consequences of the smash, and have to accept reduced damages for injuries?

Take careful note of what the Highway Code says about vehicle security. Apart from your own potential loss you carry an important responsibility in the fight against rising theft and against joy-riding and its consequent dangers to the

11

public.

At the back of the Highway Code are to be found extracts from the major Acts of Law which relate to driving. Although printed in small type it is vital to know them.

The examiner will watch your driving to see that you uphold the *spirit* of the Code; that is, you always show consideration for other road users.

Learners who pass their Test with automatic transmission are then restricted by their licence to automatic-geared cars. The opposite however, does not apply. So a manual-gear licence (as are the majority) is the more flexible option.

When you have passed your Test I hope you may be interested in my sequel to this book, which is also a *Paperfront* and is called 'Very Advanced Driving'. In it you will find a wide-ranging extension of the good driving this book attempts to teach, with the emphasis on further developing "instinctive" safety.

Both my books were first written long before attempts at distorting the English language in respect of sex became fashionable, or indeed were aided and abetted by the long arm of the law. Rather than mutilate words like *manhole* cover I hope that readers will bear with me, and understand that whenever I use the word *he* I mean also to include reference to women.

I hope readers will want to share my gratitude to Tim Barnard for his care, patience and inspiration producing the cover design and the illustrations.

A.T.T.

PART ONE

LEARNING TO HANDLE
THE CAR

HOW TO SIT

HOLDING THE WHEEL
Figs. 1 and 9 show you how to hold the steering wheel. Keep your thumbs towards being along the inside surface and grip lightly around the wheel-rim with the fingers.

ADJUSTING and SECURING THE DRIVING SEAT
With the seat adjusted properly your knees and elbows will be roughly half bent. You will find that you can easily depress any of the foot pedals to its *fullest extent*. The gear lever will be comfortably to hand.

The clutch foot pedal is the left hand one of the three. Perfect clutch control is essential for a **Smooth Start From Standing,** as will soon be explained. The art of gaining it is to make sure, whilst you use the clutch pedal during this process, that your left heel *remains on the floor*, where it can act as a pivot. Bear that in mind as you adjust the seat. Otherwise **Smooth Start** clutch control will have to come from your thigh muscles which is much more difficult. Never drive in sling-back high-heeled shoes, flip-flops or loose-fitting open-toed sandals etc. Safety demands the positive feel of well-fitting shoes.

It is dangerous to sit slumped in the seat with outstretched legs. You lose forward vision, especially near the car. You distort your impressions of distance. If you have to brake hard you may lack the ability, your leg already being too straight. Short people may need a fitted seat cushion or a properly made backrest in order to sit up right. In some cars an adjustable steering wheel position helps solve any prob-

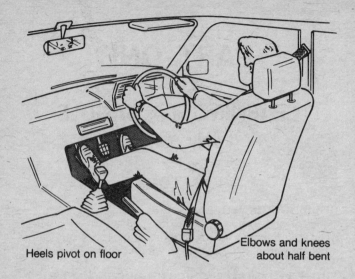

Heels pivot on floor

Elbows and knees about half bent

Fig. 1 How to sit.

lems. Be sure to lock it after a change.

Make *certain* that your seat is secure after adjustment. Were it to slide back or drop down as you braked, your push on the footbrake could be ineffective – a potential killer.

Always wear loose-fitting clothing so that you are comfortable, at ease, and unrestricted.

HOW TO ADJUST THE MIRRORS

Fig. 2 shows proper mirrors' coverage. Sitting normally, with the car on level ground, your centre mirror should capture the view through the whole back window. Check how the anti-dazzle setting works if this mirror has one. Each door mirror adds to that view immediately alongside and behind the car as shown. Aim them parallel with level ground to maximise distance seen. There is little point in adjusting any mirror unless it is spotlessly clean. Treat them like the family silver ought to be. Let haze or fingerprints blot out your view at your peril.

Fig. 2 Mirrors adjustment. Note how the "blind" areas shaded cannot be covered. Vehicles often remain hidden almost alongside you (though slightly behind) – even big lorries. To your front substantial dangerous blind spots are caused by the roof pillars. Tall people may find a similar, and very important, problem is caused by the interior mirror.

FINDING THE CONTROLS BY TOUCH AND FEEL

With the car adjusted for *you* your next task in **STAGE ONE** is to understand the *main* controls. Then to practise working them *without running the engine* and WITHOUT LOOKING DOWN. To start with your teacher should show you how. Then you can practise on your own – but make sure you never let the handbrake off unless you have the footbrake on and a gear engaged! You would be responsible for a runaway car.

This will be of tremendous benefit later, because muscles and reactions become experienced and get "into the groove".

As well as the foot pedals, gears and handbrake, you must also be able to operate the important switches – all the lights,

15

headlamp dipswitch, wipers, windscreen washers, horn, flashing indicators, heating/demisting controls and so on – *by touch or feel*.

Many drivers, now dead, would be alive if they had learned to use their eyes for the road only. If a cyclist looks down at his front wheel he soon hits something. Pain and twisted front wheels teach him to take a longer view. Keep *your* eyes on the road.

THE FOOT PEDALS

They are from your left, the clutch, brake (usually similar in appearance) and accelerator. The accelerator and brake are used with the *right* foot, the clutch with the *left*.

Fig. 3 illustrates the use of each pedal. The clutch is further explained shortly.

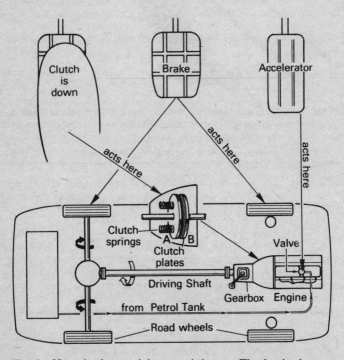

Fig. 3 How the foot pedals control the car. The footbrake acts on all wheels at once.

For a car with automatic transmission refer to page 183 but study this section to gain a working knowledge of ordinary car control.

WHAT THE ACCELERATOR DOES

To drive the car at varying speeds the engine must be fed with the right amount of petrol. Faster driving needs more. A regulating "valve" between the petrol tank and the engine is therefore provided. This may be a carburettor, or fuel-injection may be used. Either way it is controlled by the accelerator pedal.

Pressing the pedal opens the valve to speed up the engine. The pedal is spring-loaded so that the valve will be closed again as soon as you release the pedal. It will return the engine to the lowest possible speed ("ticking over") whenever your foot is off the accelerator. The light spring-loading against your foot makes it easy to maintain any constant speed or to speed up or slow down, at will.

PULLING POWER

Engine speeds vary from about 1,000 to around 6,500 revolutions per minute (r.p.m.). Fig. 4 shows diagrammatically how the average engine only gives its best and most economic pulling power (or torque) between a limited range of r.p.m. In order best to use this range the speed of the engine rotation has to be geared to the speed we want the wheels to turn and the car to go.

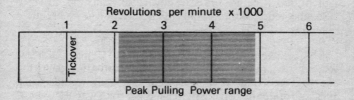

Fig. 4   Engine pulling power.

THE GEARBOX

Most cars have 4 or 5 forward gears. 1st, or bottom, gear is for starting from standing and is used up to 10–15 m.p.h. (miles per hour); a 2nd and 3rd gear are necessary for increasing speed and/or to give extra power for climbing steep hills; and a 4th, or top, gear is required thereafter. 5th is usually a fuel-saving cruising-speed gear rather than for acceleration. The gearbox is normally bolted to the engine block, with the clutch situated between the two as in fig. 3. The gear (selection) lever will either locate directly into the top of the gearbox as shown, or may be "remote", using some form of interconnecting system between the gear lever and the gearbox. This merely depends on the layout of your engine and transmission and makes no difference to driving the car.

Reverse is selected by the same lever. This gear reverses the direction of rotation of the driving shafts and thus moves the car backwards.

A neutral position, where no gear is engaged, is provided, so that you can use the gear lever to take the car out of gear. The engine can then be run without moving the car.

WHAT THE CLUTCH DOES

Engaging gear to start off, or changing gear as you go along, would be difficult without disconnecting the engine whilst the different gear cogs are meshed together.

To enable this we have the clutch. It is designed to give a *smooth* transfer of the drive (or power) from the engine to the road wheels as you connect or reconnect that drive by using it.

Fig. 3 shows how the clutch consists of two circular plates facing each other. Here, they are shown separated by the clutch pedal being pressed down, so that the drive is disconnected – as if for the initial selection or subsequent changing of a gear.

The principle is simple. Plate **B** in fig. 3 spins with the engine at whatever speed it is running. Plate **A** is attached to the gearbox, and, if a gear were engaged, would, when turned, rotate the driving shafts and the road wheels to move the car. This plate **A** only turns if you allow the clutch pedal to come up again, when the strong springs shown behind force it against plate **B**. Once it reaches plate **B** and locks against it the two turn as one, taking the drive from the engine. Unless you are in neutral that drive then passes on through the gearbox – geared according to the gear selected – to the wheels.

Plate **A** approaches plate **B** under pressure from the springs but controlled by the clutch pedal as you release it.

A smooth transfer of the drive for starting off depends upon *the period when the clutch is "slipping", when the two plates are only partially engaged*. This is the period during your release of the clutch pedal which later on I will describe as the "biting point" – when plate **A**, beginning to bite against plate **B** which is already turning, starts to turn slowly itself, building up speed as it locks more tightly with plate **B**, until it too is turning at engine speed.

Careful control of your clutch pedal release at this stage, is what makes sure the connection occurs gently and progressively. Thereafter, once your clutch pedal is fully released, the two simply go on turning together with no slip – the normal state when you are travelling along in gear.

A smooth reconnection of the drive as you change up or down the gears once you are on the move, also depends on the way you release the clutch pedal. However, as will be explained when you come to **How To Change Gear**, it is then merely a smooth release passing through the biting point that is needed.

THE GEAR LEVER

Fig. 5 shows typical gear lever positions. The lever can only move in certain channels. A diagram of these is usually etched on the top of the gear lever knob or posted nearby.

You need to be able to visualise this "gate", as it is known, *without looking down*.

Then – *without the engine running* – you can practise selecting different gears as well as finding neutral. (In neutral the lever should move freely from right to left and back.) Practise dozens of times till you have the feel of it all, and *don't look down!* Practise till you don't need to look down whatever gear you wish to select.

Hold the clutch pedal down during this practice. This should ensure the lever can slip from gear to gear without being "sticky".

Your gearbox is made so that it should be impossible to select reverse in error. In most cars an extra push has to be made before the lever will slide along the neutral channel far enough to reach the reverse slot; sometimes a catch on the

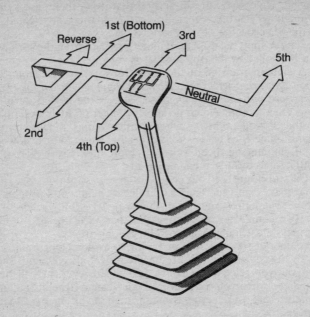

Fig. 5 Gear box gate.

lever must be lifted, or else the lever knob has itself to be pressed down in line with the lever, before the reverse slot can be selected. Check with your teacher that you understand the design.

HANDLING THE GEAR LEVER
The knob on the gear lever should snug gently into the ball of your left hand, while the fingers and thumb drop lightly around the lever lower down; it should be just like holding a cricket ball lightly, with the palm of your hand facing down. Fig. 6 shows how changing the *angle* at which your hand takes hold of the gear lever knob, enables you with precision to push, or pull, or move the lever sideways. Guide it gently. Persuade; never force. You should soon find you can change up or down the gearbox, find neutral, or select reverse – all with minimal effort and having your hand away from the steering wheel for the least possible time, *without looking*, and with neat "fluid" movements.

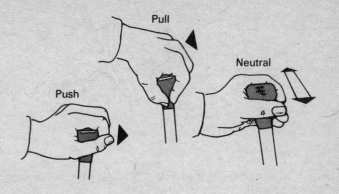

Fig. 6 Gear lever grip.

THE FOOTBRAKE EXPLAINED

Look again at fig. 3. The footbrake acts via hydraulics on all four wheel brake discs or drums at once, and is for stopping the car smoothly and progressively, or quickly in emergency.

Examine a bicycle brake and note how two pads squeeze the wheel rim, the friction created slowing the wheel. In a car the principle is similar; the brake disc (or drum with drum brakes) which turns with the wheel, is braked by lined pads being squeezed against it.

In fig. 7, **A** is the *off* position to which the spring-loaded footbrake pedal returns automatically after use. Between **B** and **D** is the point where you can feel the brakes begin to act when the foot pedal is pressed. The action is progressive. Light pressure slows the car straightaway. Gradually increasing pressure stops the car more quickly. At the first touch on the pedal your brakelights come on to warn drivers behind.

THE HANDBRAKE EXPLAINED

This works mechanically (entirely separately from the footbrake) and holds the car when standing. (You would only try to use it for stopping if your hydraulic brakes had failed. It has only a small fraction of the power of the footbrake and normally only acts on one pair of wheels.)

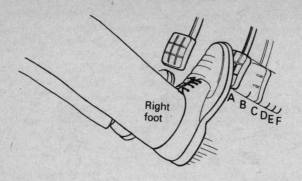

Fig. 7 Brake pedal. If it ever goes below **D** your brakes need immediate repair.

Practise "off" and "on" with the handbrake while stationary *without the engine running*, doing it by feel, and *not looking down*. So that there can be no danger of the car moving, have your foot on the footbrake and a gear engaged. Your teacher must demonstrate first, just how much strength is correct to use so as to ensure the handbrake is fully on, without overdoing it.

Normally a spring-loaded button locking device is incorporated at the end of the handle of the handbrake lever. Fig. 8 shows the commonest type. The lever has to be lifted slightly

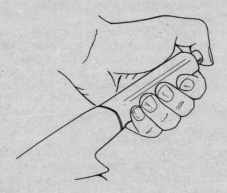

Fig. 8 Handbrake application and release button.

and the button pressed in before the lever can be moved to the down, off position. Then you release the button again.

When you pull the handbrake on press the button in first. Once the handle is fully up you release it again to lock the brake on. Amateurs who pull on the handbrake without pressing in the button cause a "click-click-click" which results in unnecessary wear to the ratchet mechanism.

In all the above **STAGE ONE** I have stressed the importance of knowing the controls by touch and feel.

OPEN SPACE PRACTICE

For **STAGE TWO** no substitute really matches a good-sized open space if you want to learn slow-speed car handling to competition standard. And that has to be your target if you want to become a first class driver! My specially devised training exercises which follow shortly can hardly be done without one. Success with them is the golden key to worry-free car manoeuvring. So do find a clear *level* open area even if it means your teacher has to drive some way to it on several occasions. Having safe room to yourselves is paramount at this stage.

Beware! I'm afraid there are a few rogue professional instructors. These chaps try to plunge you into heavy traffic practically before you have learned to move off and stop, never mind handle the car or judge its length or width. By skimping the early teaching of clutch control and manoeuvring they may hope to save wear and tear on their school car, or to prolong your lessons by slowing up your learning; I don't know. But should you find yourself in the hands of a menace of this sort look for a new instructor straightaway. There is little worse for your morale than to be driving along scared out of your wits whilst an instructor of this type keeps grabbing the steering wheel, or uses dual foot controls so much that you are constantly deprived of any real learning.

STEERING

We have not so far covered steering, because it strains the mechanism to steer while standing. This applies whether or not you have power steering. Until the instant that a car is on the move the forces that have to come into play at the steering joints would be excessive. Read about steering now before putting it into practice later.

Remember you will have to be **LOOKING WHERE YOU**

ARE GOING not at the steering wheel.

Relax! The steering wheel should always be held gently like you would hold an egg – although ready to grip harder in emergency. Steering is self-centering. That is it tends always to keep the road wheels "straight ahead". It is thus bad to grip the wheel as if force were needed to keep straight. Indeed such "conscious" steering results in a weaving wiggly course. Keeping straight is more a matter of making occasional minor corrections.

Fig. 9 shows how the steering wheel should be held between clock-face positions a "quarter to three" and "ten to two" during straight driving.

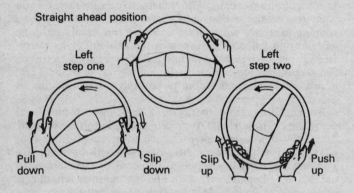

Fig. 9   Steering hand-movements.

Both hands must be on the steering wheel all the time except when one is needed for changing gear, for an arm signal, or perhaps to use a switch. **NEVER** take both hands off at once!

To alter course, very little steering wheel movement is needed, especially at higher speeds. It is only in turning at junctions, cornering acutely, reversing, and in "tight" man-oeuvring that you have to turn the wheel much. Practice will soon show you how the car responds.

When you do need to turn the wheel substantially you must *never cross your hands*. You must also learn to do it quickly. You must use two basic movements repeating them alternately as needed. These are shown in fig. 9 as steps one and two. The method avoids crossing the hands.

Fig. 9 shows turning left. To turn right do the opposite. In step one the left hand pulls down, turning the wheel; at the same time the right hand moves down, allowing the wheel to slip through its fingers so that at the end of step one both hands are level, near to the bottom of the wheel, ready to start step two.

For step two the right hand pushes up and is turning the wheel, while the left hand moves back up again so as to keep level with it, and ready to repeat step one.

Several movements may be necessary to put the steering into full lock (the wheel as far as it will go left or right).

To straighten up use the opposite hand movements. Again, speed is often necessary. Learn to be vigorous and quick, for times when you have to be. For *small amounts of steering* you may find the self-centering mechanism is sufficient but you *must not let go*, allowing the wheel to jerk back to straight. Rather must you control this self-centering action by lightly gripping the wheel as it slips back.

The steering acts on the front wheels, so immediately you turn the steering wheel (with the car moving), the front starts to turn. The rest of the car and the back wheels follow. The back wheels thus describe a smaller circle than the front ones. See fig. 10. The back of the car "cuts" the corner. On the road this effect is only important if a sharp turn is taken too close to the kerb. Then the back wheels would mount it. Don't worry over this. Once you are used to it your mind will allow room to get round, without conscious thought.

As you begin practising starts and stops on your open space, also practise steering to the left and right. Do so *before* learning to change up out of 1st gear. Later, learn to hold a straight course with the right hand only. You will need to when changing gear. Do the same with the left hand only, so that it will be possible to give arm signals.

THE SMOOTH START FROM STANDING

In figs. 11 and 12 and the accompanying text I have set down all the steps in their precise order. I assume: you are sitting correctly in the driver's seat with your seat belt on and the mirrors are adjusted for you (do them if you haven't already); the handbrake holds the car; you are holding the steering wheel in the right way (see figs. 1 and 9); you have checked all doors are properly shut – the *driver* is respons-

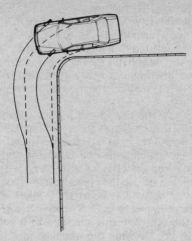

Fig. 10 How the rear wheels cut corners. Broken lines show back wheels' path.

ible. (Once you know what a door ajar looks like in your wing mirrors you can check them there.)

For the first time you will start to drive the car on your *level* open space. After practising moving off and then stopping straightaway, a few times, your teacher may need to turn the car round using reverse, so that you can go back the other way. I tend to leave reversing till after you have learned to stop competently and to change up and down the gears – so that you are generally more familiar with how a car behaves. However, there is no vital reason why you shouldn't integrate some reversing sooner. Look ahead now to **Reversing**, if you prefer.

(Note: *moving off on the road requires a signal and additional safety steps such as a check behind over your right shoulder*. I will cover them fully in **PART TWO**.)

Meanwhile:

Key to Fig. 11

1 Check that the gear lever is in neutral. *Proof* of being out of gear is that the lever moves *freely* from side to side at least twice as far as it will if it is in a gear. To help you recognise the neutral channel, if ever you are not certain, select two adjacent gears in turn, say 1st and then 3rd, next checking that you get back to neutral between them. (Have the clutch pedal down while doing this.)

If you forget the check and start the engine in gear the car might jerk forward (or back . . .) and hit somebody.

Whenever the car is to be started, or re-started if it has stalled (stopped), this neutral check must be made. On Test the examiner will watch.

Key to Fig. 11

2 Switch on the ignition (but not the engine yet) with the key. Your teacher will show you how. Go through with him the meaning of all the warning lamps which light up, and discover which ones should go out when the engine starts.

Then start the engine with a further turn of the key, now against a small but noticeable spring pressure. Immediately it runs release the switch. With practice your ear will tell you the instant the engine fires but at first your teacher can guide.

Check through the warning lamps and look at the various gauges. You need to discuss with your teacher where each one of the latter should settle once the engine is warmed up. Always check the petrol gauge. Make that a starting-up habit; later on it will help you avoid ever running out of petrol, because you will go straight to a garage if necessary.

THE CHOKE

Starting a cold engine may require the use of a choke control if an automatic choke is not fitted. This is usually a pull-knob on the dashboard, which is kept out till the *earliest moment the engine runs normally.* Then it is progressively pushed home. Your teacher must advise just how soon to begin closing off a manual choke. The skill is to do so before lumpy, "chug, chug", running occurs, but not before the engine can manage with less choke without stalling. The aim is to have it right off as soon as possible.

You must beware of leaving the choke permanently out by mistake. Even a small amount of choke can eventually flood the engine with petrol and stall it. If you keep a fingertip stretched toward the control you won't forget.

If the engine won't start don't hold the starter switch on indefinitely. That will wreck your battery. Rest a few seconds and try again with short bursts. Make sure everything electrical (other than sidelights where the law says you must

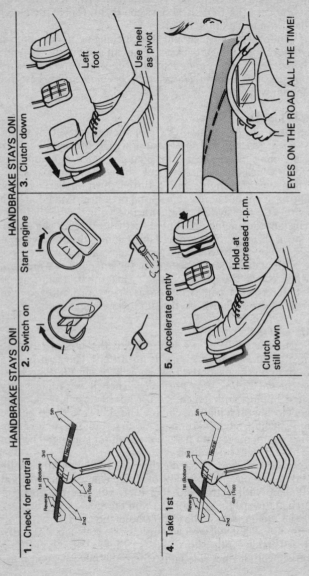

Fig. 11 Starting from standing, first **5** moves.

28

have them on at night) is switched off while you do so. Also hold the clutch pedal down; that saves turning over parts of the gearbox. If it won't go after a dozen tries seek expert help. Otherwise if you flog a flagging battery you may never get the car started.

Delve into your car handbook and find out what the recommendations are for cold starting. Each make of car seems to differ slightly. You may also find necessary tips there, for starting when your engine is hot.

Key to Fig. 11
3 Return your starter hand to the steering wheel. Put the clutch pedal fully down (left foot) *and hold it there*.

Key to Fig. 11
4 Slip the gear lever into 1st. *Return your hand to the steering wheel.*

If you find difficulty in getting into 1st, then provided your open space is flat, 2nd gear will do for starting. (When facing downhill on a road 2nd gear is correct anyway, as, helped by the decline, the engine gives sufficient power.)

Key to Fig. 11
5 Now in gear and *with the clutch pedal still down,* gently increase the engine r.p.m. Press the accelerator (right foot). About a *quarter* of its movement will be sufficient. That will be just enough for the engine tone noticeably to increase. *Hold it there.* (If your car has a tachometer you will see the engine r.p.m. rise from roughly 1000X to 1500X.)

The engine is now running at enough speed; *the clutch pedal is still down;* the gear is in 1st. Your hands are on the wheel in the correct position holding it lightly. **YOUR EYES ARE** *in front.* The handbrake has been on holding the car all the time.

Key to Fig. 12
1 and 2 The secret now is to allow the clutch pedal up only until the biting point is *just* reached, *no further.* You hold it there ready for **3** and **4**. You maintain your accelerator exactly where you set it in **5**, fig. 11 opposite.

Fig. 13 shows your clutch foot in greater detail. The clutch begins to "bite" between **B** and **D**. The exact point is not necessarily **C**; it will depend on how much the clutch plates are worn, and this naturally varies from car to car.

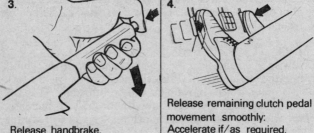

1. Allow clutch to come up to *biting point* only.

2. Listen to engine tone to guide you for 1.

Noise lessens as biting point is reached.

EYES ON THE ROAD ALL THE TIME!

3. Release handbrake.

4. Release remaining clutch pedal movement smoothly: Accelerate if/as required.

Fig. 12 Starting from standing, next **4** moves.

The master key to raising the clutch pedal to precisely where you want it and then holding it there, is (as stated earlier) *to keep your heel on the floor, where it can be a pivot.*

You can recognise the biting point because the tone of the engine's purr will die down as this stage of clutch release is reached. Let the clutch pedal up slowly so that you can't overshoot it.

Think of this point as your contact between standing and moving. To be crude, between life and death – it's that important.

The car is still held back by the handbrake, though it is now almost "straining" to go. The clutch plates as in fig. 3 are already skimming each other but only just.

Key to fig. 12
3

(a) Let the handbrake off. Then bring that hand back to the wheel.

(b) **Maintain your clutch and accelerator positions as at 1/2 above**. The car should remain still. If it creeps forward don't release your accelerator. Dip the clutch pedal a tiny fraction. 1–2 mm should be enough to stop the car without taking you back below the biting point. Again, hold your feet where they are now, with the car still. (You will know if you have dropped below the biting point because the engine tone will go up again to where you had originally set it. If that happens it is wise not to see-saw with your foot. Instead pull the handbrake back on, put the clutch pedal right down and return the gear lever to neutral. Follow by releasing the foot pedals. Next pause for breath! Then start again at fig. 11, **3**.)

(c) Now fractionally let the clutch pedal up, "slipping" the clutch to allow only enough engine power through for the road wheels to *begin* to move the car. The clutch plates as in fig. 3 are now partially engaged, carrying the car forward that ever-so-slow amount.

Key to Fig. 12
4 The more SMOOTHLY (not specially slowly) you now release the remaining movement in the clutch pedal the better.

If you jerk your foot off or raise it too quickly the car will lurch forward and the engine may stall. Let it up steadily, in control, so that the car gains speed without kangeroo hops.

Further steady acceleration as the clutch pedal passes **C** in fig. 13 – clutch now fully engaged – increases speed as required till the maximum in 1st gear is reached.

As soon as your clutch pedal is fully up remove your foot off it. There should be room to "park" your foot to the left of the pedal as shown shortly in fig. 14. If not draw your foot back towards you so that it can rest instead on the floor well clear of the pedal. Never travel with your foot still touching on the pedal. That will quickly cause undue and expensive wear on the clutch thrust bearing.

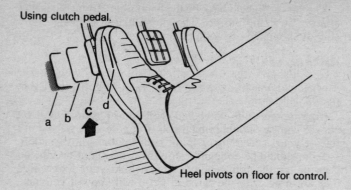

Using clutch pedal.

Heel pivots on floor for control.

Fig. 13 Clutch begins to engage between **B** and **D**.

LEARNING TO STOP

1st gear is not normally used much beyond walking speed, then 2nd is engaged, but *before* you learn to change gear on the move or accelerate strongly *you must learn to stop*.

After a few metres, *not miles*, make your first stop. Practise on your open space, starting, going a few metres and stopping, not once, but dozens of times until the "system" for stopping becomes instinctive. *It will be the life-saver later.*

STOPPING FROM *SLOW* SPEEDS

As you move your foot across from the accelerator and gently apply the footbrake the car will slow; just before stopping, the engine has to be disengaged from the road wheels or it will stall. To do so and prevent this you must put your clutch pedal down at the same time as your brake pedal. Hold it down until you have *stopped, applied the handbrake, and slipped the gear lever into neutral* IN THAT ORDER.

Keep your footbrake on till your handbrake is on. Remember that the clutch pedal must stay down till you are safely in neutral. Then you release it pending your next **Smooth Start**.

(This strict *handbrake, gear, clutch foot off* sequence must also be applied whenever you stop the engine after having parked the car. Switch off simply by turning the ignition key back to the position from which you can withdraw it.)

The rule then, for stopping from any *slow* speed, is BOTH FEET DOWN. Increasing the pressure on the footbrake progressively stops the car.

THE FEET POSITIONS

Fig. 14 shows where your feet should normally be placed after the initial start. The right foot pivots on the floor and is on the accelerator; the left lies beside the clutch ready to return to it either during the next stop, or, as will be required later, when you come to change gear.

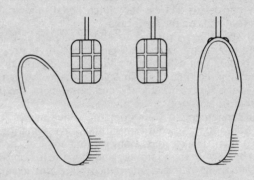

Fig. 14   Position of the feet driving along.

NEVER drive in *heavy boots*, *"wellies"*, *or muddy or greasy shoes*. Clean off mud or anything greasy. Tragedies happen in an instant. There *must never be any possibility of your feet getting "tied" up,* of one foot hitting two pedals, or of a shoe slipping off the brake or the clutch (or onto the accelerator). *In emergency, split-seconds matter.* For the same reasons never allow either foot to find its way under the pedals, and keep the footwell clear of rubbish.

EARLY EMERGENCY STOPPING FROM
SLOW SPEEDS

As soon as you get used to using the clutch and brake pedals, and you feel comfortable starting off in 1st gear and then stopping again, try an emergency stop on your teacher's unexpected snap command. (He should give it in the style an examiner would use. See page 69.) This tunes up your reactions. It ensures that your emergency drill begins to be ingrained before you ever change gear.

Later, as you learn to use 2nd and 3rd gear, reverse, etc., you must continue to practise stops, and emergency stops, in each gear, before going on. Make sure during this early open space practice, that your teacher gives you plenty of periodic snap emergency stops. You should soon be able to get BOTH FEET DOWN very, very quickly.

STOPPING FROM FASTER SPEEDS

When stopping from anything over 20–25 m.p.h. it is not necessarily correct to depress the clutch pedal immediately your other foot goes on the footbrake.

Wait till speed has dropped to about 10 m.p.h. before disengaging the engine from the road wheels by depressing the clutch pedal. You will avoid stalling provided you always have it down by the time the gear lever starts to "waggle" – indicating that a stall is imminent – and certainly by the final car length before you stop.

Another refinement to your stopping, which makes for a smoother ride, is to ease your foot off the brake again for the last metre or two. The car then stops without any jerk, before you hold it again with the footbrake and then the handbrake.

Practise stopping at a pre-determined place, for example, beside an old tree stump or whatever. You need to become expert at coming to a stop both evenly, and precisely where you decide so to do.

EMERGENCY STOPS FROM FASTER SPEEDS

However, for *EMERGENCY* stops, you can forget the "wait till 10 m.p.h. clutch pedal down rule" given above. At this stage of learning you need only remember BOTH FEET FIRMLY DOWN TOGETHER as before, as quickly as humanly possible. For stopping from any speed up to about 40 m.p.h. there is no time to think separately of when to press the clutch so you press both clutch and brake pedals at once. Fig. 15 shows you.

Even an emergency stop has to be controlled, especially in skiddy conditions. It's useless stamping on the pedal and "locking" the brakes and skidding. (Braking too hard causes "locking", a condition where a road wheel stops turning, and instead *slides*. Often several, or all, wheels slide at once.) Early in **PART TWO** I deal with how to cope with this wheels-locking problem. Meanwhile, during your open space

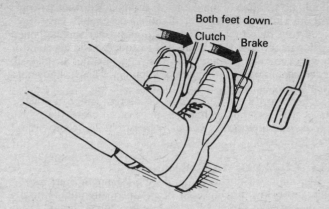

Fig. 15 Emergency stopping.

emergency stop practice, avoid wet, skiddy weather or loose surfaces. Later on in **PART TWO** I will return to emergency stopping from higher speeds, and in **PART FOUR** I investigate skidding for you in depth.

MILE-AN-HOUR DRIVING

A superb exercise for your initial live practice in **STAGE TWO** is to hold the clutch and accelerator pedals as at **Key to Fig. 12, 1 and 2**. Next let the handbrake off and drive ten or fifteen metres at "one-mile-an-hour", controlling speed for this by fractional up or down movements of the clutch pedal as required – up to begin – but holding the accelerator steady. Practise in 1st gear till you can go so slowly that it would take an observer at least a couple of seconds to be sure you were moving at all, and you will have become master of the clutch. *This clutch work is the bread and butter of learning to drive well*.

MINIMUM SPEED – CLUTCH PEDAL UP

An extension of the above exercise is to see how slowly the car will move with the clutch fully engaged (clutch pedal right up) without stalling. Return to the **Smooth Start From Standing**, figs. 11, 12 and 13. This time at **Key to Fig. 12, 4**, instead of steadily increasing acceleration after the clutch pedal is fully up, reduce it. Do so *very* gently. In 1st gear it

35

should be possible to make the car drop back down to a crawl without stalling. Thereafter it should be equally easy (provided your right foot pivots on the floor properly as explained earlier under **The Feet Positions**) to squeeze the accelerator down ever-so-gently and progressively, in order to pick up speed again without kangeroo hopping. This is known as "feathering in" your accelerator.

When shortly you come to reversing remember to practise the same essential techniques in reverse gear. It's worth discovering how slowly you can operate in *2nd* gear without clutch slip too.

CLUTCH WEAR AND TEAR

Learning to slip the clutch during a **Smooth Start** and to gain ultra-slow-moving control for manoeuvring, naturally wears out your clutch plates a few percentage points faster than normal. This is a small price to pay – for 100% competence here is essential.

However, within quite a short time, you will become able to merge the **4** steps of fig. 12 into one smooth operation – subject only to constraints from other traffic. You will learn, in the same way that all good qualified drivers do, to minimise the time that you need to hold the clutch at its biting point.

Keep **Mile–an–Hour** driving practice down to 2–3 minutes at each occasion. This will limit any undue wear. (Going on too long *at once*, may overheat the plates, which can increase the wear dramatically.) You shouldn't need very many sessions to achieve success.

Incidentally, now you are familiar with the biting point, you no longer need to press your clutch pedal "right to the floor" at every **Key to Fig. 11, 3** stage of your Smooth Start; comfortably below the biting point will do.

GEAR SPEEDS

Fig. 16 shows the speed range in which each gear is normally used.

Use 1st gear for starting and up to 10 or 15 m.p.h. However, when facing downhill, you should start in 2nd.

Use 2nd up to about 25 m.p.h. Use 3rd to accelerate between 20–25 and about 35 m.p.h. Take top thereafter for ordinary driving, until you begin learning to use 5th gear, for which see below and see **Gears On The Open Road** in PART TWO.

You would only push up toward the top speed available in each gear (broken outlines) when you want maximum acceleration, for example for overtaking.

Notice from fig. 16 that, at times when best acceleration is not needed, you can also pull away in 3rd (or even top) from as low as 10 m.p.h.

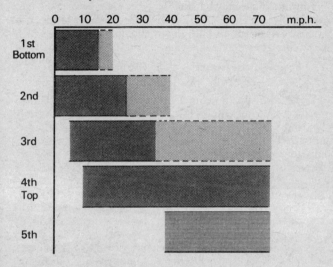

Fig. 16 Gear speeds.

On most cars there is a 5th gear. It is shown in fig. 16 with a different shading because it is not normally used for building up speed. That would take too long and hold up traffic behind. It is intended as a fuel-saving cruising-speed gear which, in addition, reduces noise and wear because the engine does not need to turn so fast.

See **How To Change Gear** below. Then practise changing up the gears on your open space. Since the engine will go on pulling perfectly adequately in 3rd and top gears from remarkably low speeds, a clear flat run of 250 metres will be ample to work your way up through the gears to top, and then to pull up. Travel a short distance with just a little acceleration in each gear. *You need never exceed 20 m.p.h.*

You will need an extended run so that you can also practise changing down again as far as 2nd gear. (Changing down to

1st gear on the move will be dealt with later; see page 78.)

HOW TO CHANGE GEAR

Fig. 17 tracks the **3** steps of changing up the gears, starting with pressing your clutch pedal down to below the biting point (there's no need for the pedal to hit the floor).

You should already be **Handling The Gear Lever** (see page 20) fluidly, WITHOUT LOOKING DOWN, after your practice earlier without the engine running.

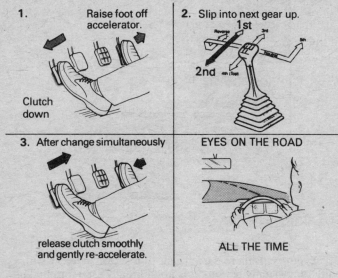

1. Raise foot off accelerator.

Clutch down

2. Slip into next gear up.

1st

2nd

Reverse   3rd

Neutral   5th

4th (Top)

3. After change simultaneously

release clutch smoothly and gently re-accelerate.

EYES ON THE ROAD

ALL THE TIME

Fig. 17 Changing up the gears.

Once you have persuaded the gear lever home confidently to select your next gear up the gearbox (fig. 17, 2), release the clutch pedal (fig. 17, 3), in one *smooth* (not slow) continuous movement.

Changing from gear to gear you do not pause while the clutch bites nor do you need to use your heel as a pivot unless preferred. You can instead lift your foot entirely off the clutch pedal using your *thigh* muscles. Either way the time it takes to say "zero" is enough.

Re-accelerate promptly after the upward change (though

progressively and not too much); don't dawdle or speed is lost.

Fig. 18 tracks changing down the gears. The **3** steps are similar to those for changing up *except that no immediate acceleration follows the change* unless the lower gear is required for extra power for climbing a hill, or for quicker acceleration to overtake someone.

A change down the gears will in most circumstances be being made in the course of slowing down. With no acceleration the lower gear will help reduce your speed through "engine braking". Instead of the engine powering the road wheels to go along, or to go faster, the momentum of the car causes those wheels to try to turn the engine faster than it is set (by the accelerator position) to go. Engine compression resistance (or "engine braking") then starts to hold speed in check and slow the car.

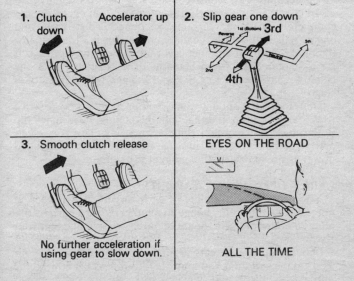

1. Clutch down   Accelerator up

2. Slip gear one down

3. Smooth clutch release

No further acceleration if using gear to slow down.

EYES ON THE ROAD

ALL THE TIME

Fig. 18 Changing down the gears.

The addition of "engine braking" helps avoid skidding and makes using your brakes safer. Going down a steep hill – especially a long one – it is a vital safety adjunct in case your brakes fade or fail.

Apart from the essential greater control afforded by the lower gears as you slow down, another reason for changing down is so that you will be in the appropriate gear ready for speeding up again just as soon as any opportunity arises.

ALMOST STOPPING . . . BUT NOT QUITE

A further exercise is to practise slowing down in 2nd gear to the point when the engine begins to falter; then, when it is about to stall, recovering to move on again without actually stopping.

You often have to do this at times when dropping instead into 1st gear would be inappropriate. For example, when turning at a level junction (with no need for the extra power of 1st), you may need almost to stop just before you enter the new road, so as to avoid any danger of swinging into it too fast.

The technique is, whilst you are still just on the move, to insert clutch-slipping, start-off control, without ever stopping completely. With the car almost stopped – just before the engine will stall – push the clutch pedal down a touch below the biting point. Simultaneously raise the engine r.p.m. as if for a **Smooth Start From Standing**. Then instantly raise the clutch to stage (c) of **Key to Fig. 12, 3** and follow directly to stage **4**.

Deft footwork should come within a very few practice tries. You will soon find that with this simple, neat, quick dip of the clutch you can slow right down at any place you select, and then have the car moving forward under controlled power again, at exactly the moment you require.

EARLY OPEN SPACE TARGETS

You now have an outline of early targets. Never keep at one exercise till tired; change to another. Most Learners tire after an hour of tuition, or at the most two, so make that your lesson limit.

Should you change cars at any time (before *or* after your Test) make sure that you know *before you set off* how all the important controls and switches work. An overtaking driver may not expect you to turn right when he sees your rear-wash-wiper come on . . . unless he is as astute as you must aim to become when you have read this book. A headlamp flash given inadvertently while trying to signal right or left can – although it ought not to (see page 151) – encourage someone to set off across your bows under a mistaken impression you are expecting him so to do.

MORE, HELPFUL OPEN SPACE TRAINING

Figs. 22–28 a few pages on, show the next few exercises to master. The ideas given create perfect conditions for learning how to place your car – to the centimetre – exactly where you want it during manoeuvring, all with zero risk of damage to your car. Obtain the necessary second-hand cardboard boxes illustrated from grocers etc. They can be flattened for transporting, and then re-sticky-taped together.

REVERSING

Apart from the steering (and the gear), all controls are used in the same way as for driving forwards.

In reverse:
You NEVER *exceed a brisk walking pace.*
You LOOK mainly **BACKWARDS** (adding necessary glances forwards and all around).
It is ILLEGAL to reverse more than necessary.
You always GIVE WAY to anyone else.

STOPPING IN REVERSE

Remember the same rule: BOTH FEET DOWN *for stopping when reversing.* Beware! Brakes are often less efficient in reversing. Allow for the difference.

YOUR EYES WHEN REVERSING

Turn well round and look out of the back window over your inside (left) shoulder. In this position you can see a little out of the windows each side as well. Get your shoulders right round as far as you can but retaining control of the foot pedals. Bend/extend your neck so that you can reduce the blind spots created by the roof supports either side of the back window. Never reverse with your head out of your side window or looking out with your door open.

Fig. 19 projects the *vital* need for developing fishy eyes for you must see all around.

When reversing straight, for example, as well as **LOOK-**

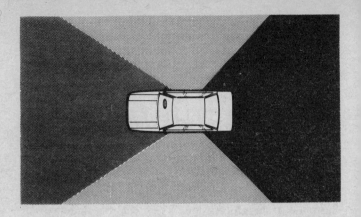

Fig. 19 Where to look when reversing. Concentrate where the shading is heaviest – you must look where you are going – but never neglect the lighter-shaded areas.

ING BACKWARDS over your inside shoulder **WHERE YOU ARE GOING,** you must move your head and switch your eyes rapidly about. You need to include frequent glances forwards, as well as to both sides – with an occasional "snapshot" right back over your right shoulder. You have to be *sure* not just that you are not going to hit anything but also that you are not causing trouble to other road users *from any direction*.

Accidents happen easily in reversing. You might be "lucky" and just hit a kerb or a low pillar but a van driver I knew killed his child by reversing "blind". *So take care.*

Pedestrians assume that you *have* seen them. Always be ready to let them pass. Especially watch for children running, perhaps crouched low after a ball . . . Should you have the slightest question as to what might be behind (e.g. at night) the Highway Code says seek help. At the least, if help is not to hand, get out first and look.

STEERING IN REVERSE

Keep both hands on the wheel. During straight reversing it may help and is acceptable to hold your respective hands on the wheel a little to the right of the top and a little to the left of the bottom, instead of the normal straight-ahead forwards position of fig. 9. However, you still use the same basic steering movements described with fig. 9. You may be told you can put your left arm along the top of the passenger seat or head-restraint. Don't. This is unnecessary if your shoulders are turned properly, and it severely reduces control.

Fig. 20 Picture this figure in your mind's-eye to remind you which direction on the steering wheel takes the car which way.

Re-study fig. 10; imagine that, rather than going forwards, you are now reversing. The path of the *wheels* is identical but reversed.

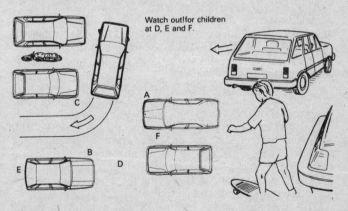

Fig. 21 Danger in a car park.

In this direction it is the back of the car, now leading, which "cuts" the corner – and the wheels at the new "back" of the car that take a wider arc. Thus the steering (or new "back") wheels are going to swing wide, and you must remember it.

In fig. 21 you are taking your position in a car park, later on, when you feel competent to do so. **A** will be an obvious front-wing danger point. So might be **B** and **C** during straightening up in the final stages of entering your "slot". Look out for pedestrians throughout the manoeuvre, especially for kids from areas **D**, **E** and **F**.

Fig. 22 shows parallel lengths of thick rope or wide cloth tape to represent kerbsides, held down by a few large stones so as to create your own straight level "road", 7–8 metres wide, 70 metres or so long, on your open space.

It is far better to be off-road; however, if you cannot find an open space big enough and have to use a very, very quiet level road instead, find a straight one where there are no parked cars and without any high kerbstones on which you might damage your tyres or wheels.

Reversing in a straight line is the first thing to learn. Nobody ever succeeds in going backwards dead straight for more than a few metres on the first attempt. They soon wander. This is because you actually learn to go straight by making mistakes and then putting them right. These errors soon diminish as you acquire the knack of keeping straight through tiny steering corrections made only when needed.

Aim to back down the full length of your "road" at a set distance out from your nearside (left) "kerb". Judge it by eye at between 1 to 2 metres out. The idea is to keep straight all the way. GO VERY SLOWLY. (Remember, in reverse you NEVER *exceed a brisk walk anyway* but this *must* be **Mile-An-Hour** stuff to begin with.)

On your first try use clutch slip for the whole distance so that you are slow enough to concentrate on exactly how your car is responding to you moving the steering wheel.

On the second go you can raise speed to a modest stroll, with your clutch pedal right up. (See earlier, **Minimum Speed – Clutch Pedal Up.**) You shouldn't now need clutch slip in this exercise except for starting off and for when you need to **Almost Stop . . . But Not Quite** (the footwork technique you learned earlier), while you rectify bad steering.

You must slow right down whilst you sort out a steering mistake. It may sound silly to slow down from a stroll to a clutch-slip speed but if you don't, you'll quickly find yourself in the "ditch".

Another exercise will impress on your mind which is the right way to turn the steering wheel to go the way you want. It is gently to weave your way back down the "road" from one side to t'other. Again, use clutch slip control all the way on your first try. (N.B. If you are on a real road you have to be able to see a *very, very long way* – to be sure that no traffic can come unexpectedly.)

A lesson or two of practice between these two exercises, combined with pulling in to the kerb backwards as part of the next exercise, will resolve all your worries about controlling your steering during reversing. As you improve at reversing NEVER go faster than my stated maximum of a brisk walk, even on the straight, and you should never scare yourself or others. Remember all the time, even on your open space, that children pop up from "nowhere". And they're liable to assume you have seen them . . .

Your "road" in fig. 22 is now the place to learn to pull in and stop (forwards and backwards) close in to the kerb. Practise mainly with the passenger's side (the nearside) of the car next the kerb. But become skilled for your side (the offside) too. An expert is able consistently to stop parallel to and within a couple of tyre-widths from the kerb, forwards or backwards, either side of the road – without ever bashing the kerb! An advanced driver such as I hope you will become, always gets it down to one tyre-width or less. His car is then less likely to get hit, or to have a wing mirror "wiped", or to inconvenience traffic in any way.

Each time you pull in and stop to begin with, get out and look how close and how parallel you are to your "kerb" with both the front and back wheels. You may be surprised to find that things are not as you thought . . . but looking for yourself is the quickest way to learn.

For the 4th exercise see fig. 23. Here you need at least 4 large cardboard cartons. On a windy day you may need a brick or two placed inside each one to stop them blowing away. Because you cannot block a public road you will *have* to find a private yard (with permission) for this and the remaining few exercises, if there is no handy open space.

Build the cartons as shown a total of one half metre wider apart than your car. Practise driving slowly between them under clutch-slipping control, forwards and then backwards. As your gap-judgment improves you will be able to go a little

Fig. 22 Your own "road" set out on an open space.

Fig. 23 Build cartons one half metre wider apart than your car.

46

quicker. Reduce the gap and test your skill at going through dead centre.

Keep the cartons where they are. Now, as shown in fig. 24, approach them from an angle before passing through. Do it forwards first, then in reverse. Your starting position should be as shown, parallel with an imaginary line joining the boxes, with the front wheels pointing straight ahead. Keep starting from positions closer and closer to the boxes – e.g. dotted lines fig. 24 – and see how good you can get.

As you work towards an ever-smaller angle you'll find you need to be progressively more adept handling the steering. Remember not to turn the steering wheel until you have the car moving; as mentioned earlier that requires undue effort from the steering gear. However, really tight manoeuvres are impossible unless you "bustle" your steering wheel rapidly round – *always using the correct basic movements learnt earlier* – from the instant you move.

A lock-to-lock turn should easily be accomplished at **Mile-An-Hour** speed *before* you have travelled one metre.

The essential success factor with this exercise is moving the car really slowly, especially when you are putting lock on or taking it off to straighten up. Loads of practice here will instil a "natural instinct" for knowing the precise best moment to start turning into your "garage" (or whatever you choose your boxes to represent), and for appreciating exactly when to begin, and how quickly, to straighten up.

As with learning correctly to pull in to a pavement be ready to stop the car and get out and look. That is the finest way YOU can learn how the picture YOU see from the driving seat relates to the facts.

It is always better to pull forwards again (but never further than necessary), and then make a correction, than to try to "get away with" a poorly executed entry, and (in a real garage) possibly scraped paintwork.

The next exercise is simpler. See fig. 25. Stand some boxes up to represent a wall. Drive slowly up to your "wall" and see how close you can get without hitting it. Use **Mile-An-Hour** clutch slip just before you finally stop, regaining that control (if you started from a long way back) as in **Almost Stopping . . . But Not Quite** a few pages ago. Do this forwards then backwards. Get out each time after you stop and see if your clenched fist will go through the gap you have left. When it won't more often than it will, you're on the way to becoming good!

Fig. 24 Discovering at just how acute an angle you can approach a narrow entrance, e.g. to a private garage.

Fig. 25 Getting to know the length of your bonnet and your boot.

If you have enough boxes or perhaps if you can procure some chest-high wooden poles and bunting as well, you can now recreate the problem of reversing into a single space in a

Fig. 26 Mock-up of a space in a multi-storey car park.

multi-storey car park. See fig. 26. Because of the bunting (or boxes) representing the front bumpers of cars parked opposite your space, you are forced to back in at a tight angle. There are plenty of "solid objects" at close quarters to worry about. You soon learn to choose your starting position with skill so that the rest becomes easy! Make up other difficult exercises too; for example, you could mock up parking between cars at the roadside, dealt with by Question 26 in **PART FOUR**. You'll never regret becoming expert at parking. And you'll never experience the fear of city-centre parking that haunts so many so-called drivers.

Figs. 27–28 show an exercise to help with the **Three-Point-Turn** which I come to next. Your length of rope or tape is shown representing the line of the gutter at the edge of a road. Drive up slowly at right angles and stop with your front or back bumper vertically above this edge.

Fig. 27 Open space exercise to teach how to stop with your bumper exactly at the kerb. Learner has here got out to double-check her skill.

Fig. 28 Same exercise as fig. 27, in reverse.

CAR CONTROL TESTS ON TEST

I now come to **STAGE THREE** of **PART ONE,** the main manoeuvring tests you will be expected to carry out on Test.

1. **THE THREE-POINT-TURN**
2. **THE REVERSE INTO A NARROW OR LIMITED OPENING**
3. **THE HILL START**

Get your teacher to drive to very quiet suitable places for each exercise. If, as I very much hope, you have been able to stay with me and keep off-road so far, remember you will now have to contend with other traffic.

1.   THE THREE-POINT-TURN

(Turning your car round between the pavements of a quiet road.)

Your teacher should find a level road 7–8 metres wide with pavements both sides, and as quiet as a cul-de-sac. Pick a spot well away from any junction and where there are no tree trunks or lamp-posts etc., to bump!

No signals are expected of you during the Three-Point-Turn so you must be especially careful about other drivers. Don't start a turn if another vehicle is approaching in either direction. Let it pass. If you are in the middle of a turn, and can wait at the point you have reached to let anyone coming go by, do so. You must expect children – up to 100 years old! – to step in front of or behind your car in the middle of your progress. Mad or irresponsible, that is their right. You stop – unless you wish to appear in Court. See PEDESTRIANS CROSSING in **PART TWO,** page 93.

The three-point or three move turn is only possible if the road is wide enough. On Test if the examiner picks too narrow a road and you need five moves don't worry. It won't be held against you. All you are expected to do is turn the car in the least possible number of forward and backward moves, without overhanging unduly, or biffing, the kerb either side and without, as far as possible, inconveniencing others.

At the start the car should be next to the kerb on your side of the road. At the finish it should be facing the other way parked next to the kerb on the other side – unless the examiner directs you to drive on as you reach the end of the final move.

Stop Properly At The Kerb

Whenever you pull in do so correctly. Your nearside

wheels should always be well within 2 tyre-widths from, and parallel to, the kerb. Set the handbrake and return to neutral. Then release the clutch.

On Test not only will the examiner be impressed by your being close in; you will be ready to begin the Three-Point-Turn. Keep your engine running after the clutch release in neutral. Relax while you listen to what the examiner wants you to do next. (The only time you switch off the engine on Test is when you finish, back at the Test centre.)

Sequence For Three-Point-Turn

In fig. 29, **1**, you are correctly pulled in next the kerb.

Check both ways that all is clear. *Turn round and look.* Do not just rely on mirrors.

When all is clear make a **Smooth Start** forwards in 1st gear at **Mile-An-Hour** speed.

Immediately the car is in motion swing the steering into full lock to take you towards the other side.

Whilst doing this make a double-check for traffic behind by looking over your right shoulder. (You can still safely stop and wait if anyone is coming.)

As fig. 29, **2**, shows, you should be *on full lock* well *before* the car has moved one metre.

Once full lock is on you can go a little quicker by releasing the clutch pedal a fraction more but you must still move *slowly* towards the other side. You should continue to keep an eye both ways for traffic as you progress.

You must slow down again by dropping the clutch pedal back down that same fraction for the last one to one-and-a-half metres towards the opposite kerb. Or, if the road banks steeply down into the gutter (which it often does), and the car starts to run on itself into the gutter, you will instead have to put your clutch pedal right down and use your footbrake to prevent it going too fast.

Fig. 29, **3**, shows this stage, still on the first lock, still under way, but where you have again slowed down to barely moving.

You are about to switch your steering fully over to the other lock (ready for the reverse back) before you stop.

During that final metre-and-a-half, *not before*, you rapidly make your lock-change. You stop – using your footbrake (and putting your clutch pedal down if it is not there already) – with your front bumper at the kerb as in fig. 30, **4**.

Your steering is already on the opposite lock (you have

just put it there). The car can overhang the kerb slightly – though not to the danger or inconvenience of pedestrians – but your tyres should not biff the kerb. (Should you fail to get the full opposite lock on before you stop, it can be completed when you start the reverse. However, you will not achieve such a neat turn.)

Next, handbrake on, gear into neutral, and look both ways, as the lady driver is doing in fig. 30, **4**, to be sure all is still clear. Wait until it is.

You now do a **Smooth Start** reverse backwards, remembering to get the whole upper part of your body, head and neck round so you can see over your inside shoulder exactly where you are aiming. All the time be alert as well for traffic coming along; if you are moving slowly enough under clutch-slipping control, you should easily be able to manage quick glances up and down the road during the period between leaving one kerb and approaching the other.

Provided you learned your **Smooth Start From Standing** properly there should be no danger of slipping forward into the gutter before you can get on the move backwards. If a steeply banked gutter causes trouble see **Hill Start** a few pages on.

Keep *fully* on this second lock till the back bumper is one to one-and-a-half metres off the original kerb. See **5**, fig. 30. The driver is *yet* to start changing back to the first lock.

Once again it is only in the last metre-and-a-half, *not before*, that you swing back to the original lock, *ready to go forwards*. Stop with the rear bumper level with the kerb as in **6**, fig. 30. Put your handbrake on again and return to neutral.

(Don't be afraid to work "furiously" with the steering wheel to achieve the lock changes. The *slower* you control the speed of the car the *easier* they are. Use the proper basic steering movements, and watch you don't cross your hands.)

Next look both ways again. As soon as it's safe drive forwards, pulling in on the other side correctly, as you did before the turn was started, unless asked to drive on. Sometimes on a fairly wide road, you will from experience realise about half way across during the backward move, that you *could* go forwards and round from there. If so, do. Likewise do so on Test; however, you are more likely then to find you need all the road available to make your turn in three moves, so do practise on "difficult" roads.

After you are confident with the **Hill Start**, and *downhill* **Mile-An-Hour** control, which come shortly, find a really

1.

2.

3.

Fig. 29 Three-Point-Turn sequence **1, 2, 3.**

4.

5.

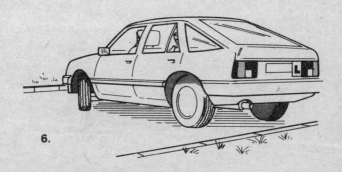

6.

Fig. 30 Three-Point-Turn sequence **4, 5, 6.**

steep hill to try a three-point-turn on. You're unlikely to get that on Test but knowing you could manage if you did does wonders for confidence!

2. THE REVERSE INTO A NARROW OR LIMITED OPENING

Your Test examiner will ask you to reverse into a limited width opening.

Most candidates are asked to reverse to the left – being the more difficult side – as in fig. 31. You can be asked to use a turning to your right as in fig. 32, so you need to practise both.

The examiner normally asks you on some *minor* road to pull in shortly after the narrow side-turning chosen, and then explains what it is he will want you to do. He may give explicit instructions about how far you are to back down the turning having entered it, or he may leave it that you are to keep going till he says stop. As you continue backing you should judge by eye to keep less than one metre from, and parallel to, the kerb on your own side (whichever that may be). Stick to that until you are ready to pull in and stop. Then move in to within 1–2 tyre-widths off the kerb by the time you reach the point requested.

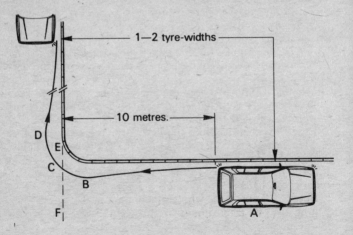

Fig. 31 Reversing into a narrow or limited opening on the nearside (passenger's side).

Find suitable quiet places, again with your teacher driving there. He should park or re-park the car safely in the starting position (**A**, figs. 31–32) each time. (Later on after experience of signalling for, and making, pull in's and turns, you will be able to do that yourself. For example, you have to be careful not to signal too early and have people think you are going directly into the turning; and you must be able yourself to select the safest point to stop.)

You must pick a perfectly flat spot for your first attempts. As will become clear, extra skills are needed if the opening or the road it leads off are on a slope. Move on to sloping terrain in due course once (up) **Hill Starts** and downhill starts and control in reverse going downhill, no longer cause you any problems.

Although you are not officially expected to give a signal during this reverse it is a better practice. So do it; give a lefthand indicator signal before you start the lefthand reverse, a righthand one before you reverse to the right. Remember to cancel the signal at the end of the manoeuvre.

Sequence For Reverse Into A Narrow Or Limited Opening

Assume you have pulled up correctly by the kerb at **A** – say 10 metres from the opening (figs. 31–32). Check for traffic from all directions. (Throughout this manoeuvre you must keep flashing your eyes *all the time* toward every avenue from which danger could come.) Then, when all is clear – including from *ahead* of you AND from *down the turning you will enter* – reverse towards **B** under superb clutch and accelerator control.

Whether doing a reverse to the left or right side, look backwards over your *left* shoulder. This makes sure you see as much as possible of the road you are leaving.

Ease the car away from the kerb straightaway but not so suddenly or acutely that one of the front (steering) wheels, *swinging wide in the first metre or so*, mounts it or rasps along it. (The latter is one of the worst treatments you can give a tyre or wheel.)

Between **B** and **D** the whole side of the car next to the kerb will need to be a maximum of 4 tyre-widths from it as you go round.

If you are doing the "easier" reverse (fig. 32, to the right side) then, as you approach and go round **B–D**, you will have the advantage of being able to glance temporarily over your

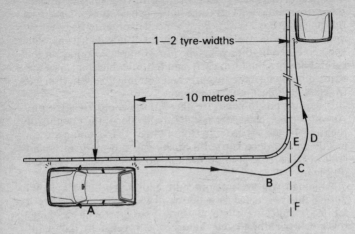

Fig. 32 Reversing into a narrow or limited opening on the offside (driver's side).

right shoulder to check how closely you are rounding the pavement.

Maintain clutch-slipping **Mile-An-Hour** control of your speed between **A** and **B**. About half way to **B** drop your clutch pedal below the biting point briefly. You will feel at once whether the car will simply stop until you move it on again by raising the clutch pedal, or whether there is in fact a downward slope which will cause the car to carry on *too quickly* into the turn. If the former happens you immediately know that, provided you don't overshoot, you will be able to **Almost Stop . . . But Not Quite** at **B**, and then continue to use your **Mile-An-Hour** technique to take you round **B–D**, and into the turning under total control. If the latter occurs – with the instant feeling the car will run away too fast into the turn – then you know you will need a *downhill* **Mile-An-Hour** technique. This simply means you are going to have to control your speed further, slow as it already is, with the footbrake (and the clutch pedal down to prevent stalling), during the critical stage from just before **B** till just after **D**.

You take charge with the footbrake for the minimum distance necessary because during that time the car is not strictly speaking being "driven". It is freewheeling. However that is unavoidable. You use a fine touch on your brake pedal during this critical period so that you never quite stop (unless you have to, e.g. for a pedestrian) but are enabled to control speed exactly as you want it. Easing the brake a smidgen lets you go faster. Restoring your pressure on the pedal checks increasing speed instantly.

Anticipation of overshooting the turn in error, despite there being no downhill slope, or perhaps recognition of a change to a downward slope on the way round, may mean you will have to combine both techniques.

Whichever way it turns out, you must be going dead slowly when you arrive at **B**. You will soon see better down the road you are to enter. There may be snags there. For example, you may need temporarily to stop, and then to move forward enough to allow someone safe vision and passage to come out of the opening, before you can go on again. (**A reversing driver always has to give way.**) Or you may misjudge, and need to pull out again a little, before you can correct your mistake. (You would move forward the minimum distance necessary before continuing; your examiner would be better pleased that way than if you carried on, foolishly, and then mounted the kerb or made a very wide entry.)

Always remember to look both ways along your original road *first* – if you do have to move forward again at any stage!

Another reason for stopping might be for pedestrians, especially tiny tots, anywhere in the close vicinity. Wait till you know what they want to do.

The line of the opening's kerbstones – if extended in your mind's eye into the road you are leaving – will, just after **B**, pass through both of your rear wheels (dotted lines **E – F** in figs. 31–32).

Check again for traffic at this juncture – glance all ways; especially watch the road you are *leaving*. If you are forced to stop, *no harm done*. As your outer front wing will shortly *swing wide*, out towards the road you are exiting, it is best to wait while traffic from *either* direction along that road passes.

From **B** onwards, still *barely moving*, you keep the car parallel to the kerb as it rounds away from you.

Swing the steering wheel into lock (as much as required – probably immediate full lock) as you move incredibly slowly between **B** and **C**. Towards **D** you start to straighten up again so that you will be able to continue your reverse, running parallel to the kerb just under one metre off it. Don't be afraid to work really fast with the steering wheel at *your barely moving road speed*, both to get your car round neatly and then to get it squared up again at the correct stage.

Now carry on at a gentle reverse pace till instructed by the examiner to pull in and stop parked by the kerbside.

It is usual to be asked to reverse several car lengths after straightening up, both to show that you can time your straightening up correctly and not overdo it, and to show that you can then back the car straight and in control. Your continued vigilance looking all around for other traffic during the extended reverse is also being watched. See **Your Eyes When Reversing,** earlier.

Unless you have been asked to pull in and stop less than three or four car lengths down the turning, your foot needs to come right off the clutch pedal during this extended reverse. Aim to have it right off immediately after you have straightened up.

Bring your foot off the accelerator at the same time, or off the footbrake if you have been restraining speed with that. Then see how fast you go on this **Minimum Speed – Clutch Up** basis (see page 35).

If you now need any additional acceleration, which you may well do, "feather" it in with a very gentle squeeze of your foot. But remember a brisk walking pace is the maximum for safety for going backwards. If you are now going downhill and beginning to go too fast despite the effect – on zero acceleration – of "engine braking" (see page 39), slow up again by braking lightly as required. With practice you will come to recognise whether you need more acceleration (or braking), with no measurable pause before you do whichever it is – indeed, almost without thinking.

If your judgment of *when* to swing into lock for these reverses is poor the answer is practice. During early attempts stop at different stages and get out and look at how your car is placed. Once you get it right this will cement in your mind how things *should* look from the driving seat. Unless you *really* are *barely moving* between **B** *and* **D** (figs. 31 and 32) there is little chance that you will get your steering right.

I mentioned earlier that extra skills are needed if your chosen side-turning is not on level ground. If the first stage of reversing towards the turn is uphill to any marked degree then ability to make a **Hill Start** (for which see below) will be essential. If going into the turning itself will still be considerably uphill, then between **B** and **D,** under clutch slip control barely moving, you will need rather more engine r.p.m. than would be needed on the level. This is akin to the extra r.p.m. that would be needed for a **Hill Start** at the same place. If, on the other hand, the slope is very much downhill to reach the turning, and goes on steeply down as you enter it, you will need to have had a reasonable amount of practice both with downhill starts which follow a few pages on, and with the *downhill* **Mile-An-Hour** technique mentioned a few paragraphs back. Hence my hints to leave more tricky reverses until you have all the control skills well "taped". Practise harder ones later on as you progress through the rest of this book.

NOTE: after a righthand reverse into a narrow or limited opening you are parked on the "wrong" side of the road facing oncoming traffic. Before you can come out again on to the road you reversed off, you first have to cross to your own side of your side-turning. You have to do this immediately you move off, using a proper left indicator signal and suitable care in the course of doing so. It is a case of adapting the full moving off procedure of fig. 36. However, your instructor should do this for you at this stage. Once you are well into **PARTS TWO** and **THREE** of this book you will be able to tackle it yourself.

3. THE HILL START
Before you can (up) hill start, understand this:

PROVIDED ACCELERATION IS SUFFICIENT TO MOVE YOUR CAR UP THE HILL, there is one point at which the clutch pedal can be held which stops your car rolling back downhill (handbrake off) but at which the gear is insufficiently engaged to move your car up the hill. With your clutch held at this point your car is "suspended" between going and rolling back.

For the level-road **Smooth Start** you already know about waiting till this biting point is reached before releasing the handbrake.

The only difference in the **Hill Start** is in the *amount* of acceleration required. More fuel is needed to make the car climb. You press the accelerator perhaps half as much again to start with **(Key to Fig. 11, 5)** as you would on level road. However, there is no need to overdo it and have the engine "scream".

Then, as your clutch comes up to the biting point and this (raised) engine r.p.m. begins to die away (**Key to Fig. 12, 1 and 2**) you hold the clutch pedal there as normally. Next, you squeeze your accelerator pedal down a tiny bit more so as to restore the higher r.p.m. you had earlier set. This brings you to the point that you are ready to let your handbrake off as in **Key to Fig. 12, 3,** (a) and (b). Do so, and you will find the car "suspended", standing still on your uphill slope. It will be ready to complete a **Smooth Start** in the normal way – **Key to Fig. 12, 3,** (c) onwards.

Let your teacher find a quiet gentle hill. Make sure there is no-one standing behind you into whom you could roll back and no-one coming along. Then experiment till you can consistently hold the car *still*, in 1st gear – neither going forward nor rolling back – when you let the handbrake off. Don't attempt to move up the hill yet.

This "initiation" practice proves that *you* (too) can "suspend" the car. (Try the same in reverse to prove you can do it that way as well!)

Once you achieve this correct "balance" between the accelerator and clutch pedals *every time*, your task is all but done. You are ready to graduate to moving off on a **Hill Start** as confidently and competently as you do on the level. Simply continue from **Key to Fig. 12, 3,** (c).

The first time you practise a **Hill Start** the car probably will run back. For this reason see fig. 33! *Stop dead with your footbrake* (and your clutch down); pull on your handbrake and then begin again. Don't accelerate wildly or jump off your clutch. *Stop and re-start*.

When proficient try the **Almost Stopping . . . But Not Quite** routine (page 40) *uphill* in 1st gear. Then see if you can slow to a *stop* using your skill with the clutch biting point alone. When you can do that – and hold it there for a second or two until *you* decide to move on – without touching your handbrake or footbrake, you can tell yourself you have truly cracked the problems of Hill Starts! Now try in reverse!

Unless a **Hill Start** occurs on Test due to an uphill queue or because of having to stop at a junction on a steep incline, you are likely to be asked to pull in at the left on a steep uphill so the examiner can check your skill. When he says "drive on when you are ready", the full moving off procedure, shown by fig. 36 and described by text there in **PART TWO** must also be followed.

Fig. 33 Hill Start. Practise first on slight inclines then progress to steeper hills.

FURTHER MATTERS OF CONTROL

You need to know about two more, important aspects of making use of engine compression resistance – i.e. *engine braking*:

SMOOTH START DOWNHILL

In **Key to Fig. 11, 4,** and later, I said 2nd gear is correct for moving off downhill. I can now add that downhill you omit raising your engine r.p.m. from your **Smooth Start** procedure. As the decline is going to cause the car to roll forward on its way anyway, directly you release the handbrake, the process from **Key to Fig. 11, 4** onwards also changes. It becomes more like the latter part of changing gear. (See fig. 17 and **How To Change Gear.**)

Assume you have selected 2nd gear, your foot holds the clutch down and you are ready to release the handbrake. Leaving aside for the moment safety procedures when moving off (to be dealt with by fig. 36), all you now need to do when you decide to go, is to let your handbrake off and then release your clutch in one smooth movement no more than an instant later – as soon as the car is on the move.

Depending how steep the decline is you can then follow up

straightaway with gentle initial acceleration, or you can allow the engine braking of being in 2nd gear, to hold the car back from increasing speed more than you want.

On a *very* steep hill you might soon need to add your footbrake to control speed to a safe level.

All the above technique avoids the car ever *freewheeling*; that is, running forward with your clutch pedal still down and therefore having no gear engaged. That would put unsafe reliance on your brakes. Apart from the very short distances when freewheeling sometimes cannot be avoided in reverse (see page 59), it is not allowed.

HILL PARKING

When you park on a hill you must first be parallel to the kerb with your back wheels about one tyre-width out from it. Then you can gently run the steering wheels in, on lock, to touch (but not to press) the kerb, before you firmly set the handbrake.

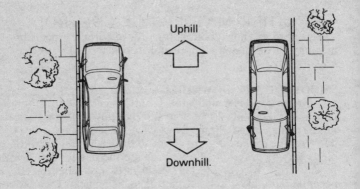

Fig. 34 Parking on a hill.

Turn the steering wheels as shown in fig. 34 so that if the handbrake were to fail, the car should quickly be stopped by the kerb. Note the difference between facing uphill and pointing downhill.

Facing uphill, leave the car in 1st gear after you switch off, to add engine compression hold; on a downhill slope leave the gear in reverse. Leave automatic transmission in the **Park** position facing uphill or down. This locks engine and transmission together to give the same effect.

Always lock doors so that children cannot tamper. See also page 11, and Questions 18, 22, 26, 32, 40, 44, 49 in **PART FOUR.**

PART TWO

GENERAL ROAD AND TRAFFIC DRIVING

BEGINNING ON THE ROAD

To pass your Test there is no substitute for thousands of miles of experience. Seize every opportunity but don't overdo it; a little over an hour at a time is quite enough on the road to begin with. Tiredness kills. (If the tiredness factor in most road-accidents could be measured it would blow the breathalyzer into insignificance.)

You will be ready to progress to the open road as soon as you are confident and competent with all the car control set out in **PART ONE.** But first – homework!

You need to know the written and unwritten rules of the road, now. Otherwise you will certainly meet a tricky situation with no knowledge of who should do what. That would be dangerous. So study the rest of this book before driving on. Then, should your teacher ever have to "rescue" you with a guiding word, you will be quick to understand.

RUNNING COMMENTARY

Get your teacher or friends to explain as they drive why they do what they do. Learn how they anticipate every course of action of their own and those of other people. Which are the dangerous situations? Why? What speeds are safe when? How early do you begin positioning for turns? Where and why do you need to change gear, or start braking, or give signals?

You will soon see how you need to think ahead *all the time* and appreciate how the driver dare not look at the scenery. That all-too-common fault invites death.

CONCENTRATION

If you have other things on your mind stop driving!

Although your mind must never wander, your aim must be to achieve relaxed concentration. Tenseness increases with tiredness so you need to come to your lessons fresh. Beware of over-concentrating, so that your teacher's comments, or *commands*, pass unheard.

NOTES FOR TEACHERS

Within *some* families the attempt to teach can turn out to be catastrophic, so you must be honest with your own and let an outsider take over if necessary.

When a difficulty needs explanation draw in to the side, traffic permitting, and discuss it there in safety. Try to do this *before* any new type of problem is tackled. Always do it as soon as you can after any incident with which you are not entirely happy.

After dealing with any such matter always ask your trainee *to explain it back to you* so that you can be certain how well things are being understood. Remember, before each new traffic complication, that you are having to assess continuously exactly where your particular pupil's reactions may be slow or his judgment *wrong*.

Do extend your Learner's experience gradually. Plan your routes. It is unnerving for him to sail into heavy traffic at the outset. It is also thoroughly selfish of both of you to create long queues behind. The frustration and anger caused may lead to accidents.

MIRRORS

Have another look at **How To Adjust The Mirrors** early in **PART ONE**. Correct mirrors' watching is an art to be developed. However, whilst you must aim always to know what is behind – to maintain a running picture – **LOOKING WHERE YOU ARE GOING** must always take precedence.

You have to learn to flick your eyes to each mirror to gather the whole position, with your *eyes back on the road* betwixt every glance; see fig. 35.

Never gaze at a mirror. You'll soon hit something if you do. There's no need to know how attractive the driver following is, only if a vehicle is there and how close.

A good teacher will ask you from time to time what is behind. If you cannot answer without another look, you are below standard. Equally he will warn you at once if he senses that you are becoming over-preoccupied by the mirrors.

Keeping your running picture of what is going on behind

enables you to position and adjust speed accordingly, so that traffic following will always know your intention in good time.

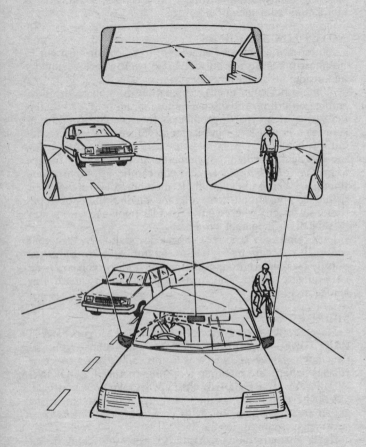

Fig. 35 Split-second mirror glances behind.

The Highway Code rightly emphasises **Mirrors – Signal – Manoeuvre.** I go further. I say **Mirrors – Mirrors – Mirrors**, manoeuvring or not. My "continuous picture" is what should save you from being caught out by people hidden in mirrors' blind spots (see fig. 2) for they can be hidden for a surprisingly long time – even for miles believe it or not; it should also alert you whenever someone wants to overtake or pass to your inside; and it forewarns you when it will be wise to position, alter speed, and/or signal, earlier than usual, for example, before moving out to pass a parked car. In emergency, when there may be no time to look again, you already have the rear view in mind.

I shouldn't have to say, but I will, that swinging dollies, stickers on the back window and a rear parcel shelf piled high with gubbins are all menaces. They merely demonstrate to others how little you know about driving.

The Highway Code demands that you do not brake sharply *except* in an emergency. But suppose you *have* to stop suddenly and are then hit behind? In Law that driver has to be to blame.

A basic Code dictum enshrines that Law: *NEVER* **DRIVE SO FAST THAT YOU CANNOT STOP** *WELL* **WITHIN THE DISTANCE YOU CAN SEE TO BE CLEAR.**

The rule is sacrosanct.

If the driver behind is any good such a bash ought never to happen. But what if it is all set to do so and the potential whiplash could break your neck? Then my **Mirrors – Mirrors – Mirrors** drivestyle should make sure you know the imminent danger: you might be able to drive clear to reach the safety of a grass verge . . . you might manage to warn passengers to tuck heads below seat-back level . . .

EMERGENCY STOP ON TEST

The examiner will pre-arrange with you a signal for when he wants you to demonstrate a SAFE emergency stop. For example, the instruction arranged may be slapping the dash board at the same time as saying STOP! You need plenty of practice, using a similar signal, so that you learn to react as fast to a contrived emergency as to a real one. Your teacher must make a point of giving you at least one emergency stop on every lesson (although only in dry weather to begin with) until satisfied you are always on the ball. He must – as you can be certain the examiner will – always have checked physically (not just in a mirror) that you are clear behind.

Your mirrors' running picture should mean you also know it is clear but even if not, you don't check the mirrors again; the instant you get the signal – *both feet down firmly and stop.* Keep the steering straight and maintain a controlled grip on it until you have stopped completely. Once stopped, hand-brake on, gear out, clutch pedal up and footbrake off. But be ready. The examiner will be telling you almost straightaway to drive on. (He can't have you sitting there obstructing the road!) Then follow **Moving Off** which I come to next, except that you don't signal, or need to move out (as in item **6** of fig. 36).

Under **Emergency Stops From Faster Speeds** in **PART ONE** and until now, I have taught you **both feet down** for any emergency stop from moderate speed. As it is normal for the **Emergency Stop on Test** to be carried out in a built-up area subject to a low speed limit, this is fine. Your reaction speed, one keynote of what is being tested, is the first essential thing that needs to become ingrained. Once it is and you have greater confidence, then is time enough to learn to leave putting the clutch down until you have almost stopped, as in a normal pull up. This shows greater skill, and needs learning for real emergencies from higher speeds because engine braking can then be a marginal extra help to you in stopping. However, if in the excitement of the **Emergency Stop on Test** your clutch goes down a little early in relation to the stopping, it won't count against you, providing your stop is quick.

To be SAFE and *in control* are the other keynotes the examiner looks for. Your car mustn't just skid all the way to a halt! In **PART ONE** I promised to return to the problem of skidding because of "locking" your brakes. Keeping your steering straight is as much part of this as it is to hold you on course, because your front wheels are more likely to lock easily if they are on the turn.

If your wheel(s) lock and skid, your brakes must be freed off at once momentarily; then they must at once be reapplied as hard as possible without re-locking them. In practice – unless you have anti-lock brakes – they tend swiftly to lock again, so this becomes virtually an on-off-on process as fast as your brain can switch the instructions to your feet.

The right technique must be learned in *dry weather* first. In **PART FOUR, Skids When Braking Hard,** I suggest an exercise to help you master it. On dry you can tell at once when a wheel is locking. The tyre screeches. Thus you know instantaneously when you must ease your brake for a split-second. Later on when you come to practise on the wet you will hear the tyre "hiss" instead, as it slides – again, warning you to ease your foot off a trice, before resuming as much

70

braking as you reckon you can, and so on.

Open your window. Then you can hear exactly when skidding starts.

In cars fitted with anti-lock brakes none of this foot-skill is needed. The system does it all for you. It senses whenever a wheel locks and temporarily releases the brake pressure to that wheel accordingly; all you have to do for the quickest stop is keep your foot firmly on the footbrake. If you are learning with anti-lock brakes you must still understand what drivers without them have to do. You may one day have to drive a car built before they were available. And you may be asked about locked-wheel skidding on your Test.

MOVING OFF
Key to Fig. 36

Follow the sequence of fig. 36. Define "clear" as when you can safely go without anyone else having to take evasive action of any kind, no matter how slight.

Give your right indicator signal during **2, 3, 4** and **5** to warn other traffic. As "other traffic" includes every vehicle ahead or behind and pedestrians, it is best always to signal in case there is anyone you haven't noticed. It is safer that way unless you are *certain* there is no-one about. If you choose to use an arm signal as well (or have to because of failed indicators), do so during **4**. The right turn arm signal is the correct one. See page 145. Return your hand to the wheel before **5**.

As the above signal may be the first "live" one you have ever had to give (apart from at my suggestion for some of the CAR CONTROL TEST reverses in **PART ONE**), I must now stress *the most essential fact* about *any* signal you make. Your indicator or arm signal is only a warning of your **INTENTION**. It does not bless you with *permission* to carry out the manoeuvre. Whether you can now do what you want to do once you have signalled, will depend upon all the other *Rules of the Road* which apply in that particular situation. These will all become clear as you read on.

Never let your car move forwards during **4**. You will see idiots do this while still looking backwards . . . Wait till you *can* go, at **6**, *after* you have double-checked ahead at **5**. At **5**, look out especially for pedestrians who may have stepped immediately in front of you by then. Believe me or not, they *will*! And beware of traffic having now pulled up just ahead

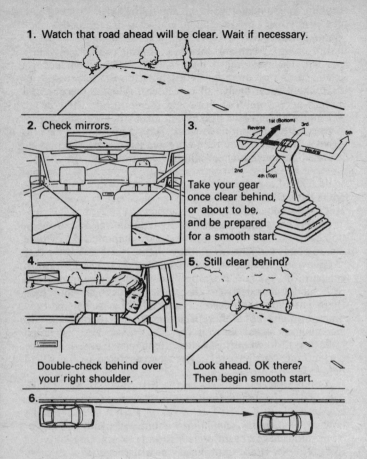

1. Watch that road ahead will be clear. Wait if necessary.

2. Check mirrors.

3. 1st (Bottom) 3rd 5th
Reverse Neutral
2nd 4th (Top)
Take your gear once clear behind, or about to be, and be prepared for a smooth start.

4. Double-check behind over your right shoulder.

5. Still clear behind?
Look ahead. OK there? Then begin smooth start.

6. Aim to reach normal distance from kerb gradually, not sharply.

Fig. 36 Moving off from a kerbside. Use a right indicator signal. Remember to cancel it.

of you, either next to the kerb or because a queue has formed.

At **6**, whilst your *moving out from the kerb* should be at a gentle angle (and you must remember we drive on the

LEFT!), your *picking up speed* should be smart (though not ferocious!).

You must acquire two more, moving-off *habits*: 1) to begin that **Mirrors – Mirrors – Mirrors** drivestyle of a few pages back straightaway. It's a favourite unexpected moment to find someone on your back bumper for whom perhaps to make allowances. And 2) to cancel your signal as soon as you are off.

If, after your road checks at **4** and **5**, something has cropped up making you have to wait for more than a moment or two, return to neutral and release your clutch pedal. Sitting at-the-ready for too long will cause undue wear on the clutch. Also cancel your signal for the time being. Renew the signal and take up **Smooth Start** preparedness again (from **3**, fig. 36), as soon as a fresh opportunity is about to arise.

When starting from behind another parked car you have no choice but to pull out more sharply (and therefore slowly, too) than in **6**. Depending on how sharp the angle is you may *also* need to wait because of *oncoming* traffic. Because the manoeuvre is more difficult the examiner will be sure to test you on it. So practise frequently. If you have any problems being certain that you won't bump the back corner of the car you are pulling out round, go back to the cardboard box practice of **PART ONE!** But remember that hitting an oncoming car is the more dangerous possibility. You must allow too, for the extra time that going slowly and having to straighten-up once you are out, is all going to take.

DISTANCE OUT

In the UK the basic rule for going along any road is that we *drive on the left*.

Where exceptions can apply – for example in one-way streets – the change of status of the road is always marked.

On ordinary single-carriageway two-way roads keep your car well within your own lefthand side of the road. Unless you have to be closer because the road is narrow, half a metre out from the kerb as a rough guide, is about right for most situations.

It is a mistake to drive permanently so close to the edge that your tyres pick up stones and debris. (Once embedded in a tyre a flint or a nail can cause a puncture thousands of miles later. If you drive stupidly close there is also danger to pedestrians and of hitting the kerb, and – even at slow speed – of losing control, as well as a chance of bursting a tyre or damaging your steering.)

Equally, it is wrong to hug just left of the centre line of the road, risking a bash with traffic going the other way, and making it more difficult or even dangerous for anyone to overtake you. That is the behaviour of a road-hog. Help overtakers by travelling no further out than you need to do.

You must relate your distance out to your speed and to the general conditions too. For example, on a wide urban road, even though going slowly because of them, you might sneak a little more out where pavements are crowded with people; on a country major road a little more than the half metre would certainly be wise above 40–50 m.p.h.

If there isn't comfortable room within your own side to add safety with extra distance out, you can bet that your speed ought to be lower instead:

—*In any emergency even a few centimetres further out can yield critical extra vision, and reaction time.*

—*Equally, religiously lifting your foot off your accelerator whenever space is tight, can mean the difference between life before death and life thereafter.*

In the left lane of a road with more than one lane in your direction, or a dual carriageway, a middle-of-the-left lane position is usually fine. As you will see shortly the left lane is where you would normally drive. (When you use other lanes a middle-of-the-lane position is normal too.)

PULLING IN ON THE LEFT

As this manoeuvre is a virtual certainty after **Moving Off** – and probably quite soon thereafter – you have to do your homework beforehand! It will be up to you to select a *safe position*. In your Highway Code is an extensive list of places where you *must not* wait or park. Be sure you know them. At first confirm too, with your teacher, that the spot you are choosing is safe.

In **PART ONE** you practised the mechanics of stopping your car closely adjacent to a kerbside. Now, you must also follow the correct pulling-in sequence.

First, check in your mirrors. Then select your safe pull-in position. How far ahead that will be also depends on your speed and on what is behind you. At 25 m.p.h. it could be as close as 50 metres. At 50 m.p.h. several hundred metres may well be necessary. You must rule out absolutely any wild "dive" for the edge such as you will sometimes witness. Such driving is dangerous.

74

Next, signal your intention with your left indicator so that everyone around (not just those behind) will know what you are up to. Double-check that people behind, if they were close, have noticed! (You can always delay your pull-in if necessary.) Then slow down gradually, timing it so that you can be/are down into 2nd gear for final control as you draw in to the edge. Unless you are only stopping for a moment, cancel your left indicator.

Should you decide to add a left-turn arm signal, which would *be the correct one for pulling in* and can sometimes make your intended stop more obvious to others, give it just after putting on your left indicator. It's worth practising too, in case your indicators ever fail. See page 145.

HOW FAST SHOULD I GO?

On Test, wherever safe, keep up to a reasonable speed. You can be failed for dawdling at 20 m.p.h. for no reason. So generally keep up with the traffic stream (unless it is too fast . . .). *Never* exceed a speed limit however (other than momentarily in error), or the examiner must fail you for wilfully breaking the law. Exceeding about 50 m.p.h. at any time on Test would none-the-less probably be unnecessary and unwise.

Always await a safe moment to check your speedometer (or any other instrument). You should soon learn the "feel" of the various speed limits so that an untimely diversion of your attention – even of a split-second – need never occur.

After passing your Test the temptation to go faster on the open road gets stronger! Unless there is more room still (than suggested under **Distance Out** a few pages back), forget it. You need to be at least a metre off the kerb on the average open trunk road before 60 m.p.h. may be safe. More than that isn't often available; which makes some sense of why we have a "blanket" 60 m.p.h. maximum speed restriction on all single-carriageway roads. Keep higher speeds for dual carriageways or motorways. At high speeds a car is many times more difficult to control, *especially to steer or stop*, so extra room is essential. Just as essential is experience. Even 100,000 miles' driving only gives you but a soupçon of that, though you may not believe me till you have driven that far.

Faster cornering, even allowing that you may be able to see that there are no traffic reasons around a bend to preclude it, carries the obligation fully to understand skidding. That, and proper cornering techniques, I come to under SKIDS in

PART FOUR. But even slow cornering demands the right approach. So please study that section early on.

DUAL CARRIAGEWAYS

Stay roughly in the middle of your lane except when changing lanes. With thick traffic in front of you on a dual, you can sometimes usefully move a tiny amount off-centre to help you see ahead but only when your mirrors and the road width allow.

Whether a dual (or any road with more than one lane in your direction) is divided into 2 or 3 (or more) lanes the first rule is that you drive in the lefthand lane except when overtaking (or turning off to the right). This matches the Highway Code rule that you always allow others to overtake you if they want to.

After you yourself overtaking (which I come to later), the second rule is therefore that you must normally return immediately to the lefthand lane, moving across one lane at a time if need be. If no one ahead of you is holding you up, then blocking an outer lane unnecessarily by just "sitting" in it (even if you are going at the speed limit) is an offence. Those behind will not unreasonably, if they wish to pass, hoot or flash their lights to tell you.

Tied in with these twin rules is the fundamental rule on all mutiple-lane carriageways (and anywhere more than one lane forms, marked or not), that you overtake only on the right except:

- when there are queues and your (left) lane goes first
- to pass to the left of someone slowing down to turn right
- to turn left yourself whilst an outer lane is – at that particular time – having to wait for some reason
- if you are in a designated one-way street and wish to pass on the left.

It is illegal (other than in a one-way system) to overtake on the left solely because someone is in your way. He is probably blocked behind others anyway, all waiting to take their turn to get ahead. In law the fact that there may be someone up front who is wilfully obstructing instead of moving in makes no difference.

In theory the third rule should make it safe to follow the first two. When you want to move back in (perhaps because it has become obvious that you will be blocked ahead indefinitely or perhaps when forced to move in suddenly) you should never have to worry that someone will be belting past on your left, whether they are in a left lane or even a middle lane of 3.

In practice, with burgeoning traffic filling our roads to capacity, you have to worry very much that that will be happening. Some people's definitions of queueing or waiting seem nowadays to range up to 70 m.p.h. plus! How *the law* might define them you must judge for yourself but I am sure that in this matter it would not be the proverbial ass.

Your main protections from such illegality lie in having a **Mirrors – Mirrors – Mirrors** drivestyle and – if ever there is someone lurking behind to your left of whose intentions you cannot be sure – in using a left indicator briefly beforehand. Add to these a flash-look over your left shoulder before you move in. This extra tip will often save you from those mirror-hoppers who seem purposely to lie in wait unseen, apparently just looking for a deadly chance to rip past you on the inside.

COUNTRY LANES

Paradoxically the narrowest lanes, where two cars cannot easily pass one another in opposite directions anyway, seem to be safer than those of middling width. On the former even lunatics go slow. On the latter quite sane drivers seem prone to chance it, cutting the corners and speeding far faster than in reality they could stop if someone came hurtling in the other direction at the sort of speed they are doing themselves. There seems to be an illusion of safety about these minor roads, yet, when accidents happen on them, they are rarely minor.

At "blind" corners and brows of hills particularly, you simply must be able to stop come what may. That may be a countryman running late who rarely finds anyone on "his" lane; it may be a lone pedestrian hidden on your side right at the apex of a corner and met just as a maniac driver springs forth in the other direction; it may be an idiot charging the other way too fast and attempting to circumnavigate a pedestrian who had been similarly concealed from him; or it may be a herd of cows, or a tractor/trailer bulging with hay. Anything can happen including the incredible.

You must discipline your speed on the basis the incredible **WILL HAPPEN**.

If say, through speeding along a winding, narrow, roller-coaster road, you killed a child "chickening – out" across it on roller skates, as quickly as you might swat a fly, WOULDN'T YOUR CONSCIENCE BLEED FOR LIFE?

You may feel I exaggerate with these examples. I hope you won't any longer after your first scare.

On country lanes keep in to your side closer than usual. Keep slow, always just a bit slower than instinct would dictate, and hopefully you should always find you have some accident evasion margin when trouble strikes, as inevitably it will. Never be bullied by people behind or "back seat drivers" urging you on. Never cut corners. Evidence that you had done so would leave you "without a leg to stand on" in the event of an accident.

Blind "single file" hump-back bridges, often incorporating a bend, can be a death-trap. Slow right down as you approach, keeping well in to your own side and ready to stop at once. Until you can see over the brow you must be going slowly enough and watching for the instant the roof of an approaching vehicle may appear, so that you can stop – and possibly hoot, too – at that second.

Various signs may dictate who has priority but they are hard ones to remember which means what. So, whilst making sure you know them from the Highway Code yourself, assume other drivers may get it wrong. Otherwise I know of no ruling as to who must give way apart from courtesy. It makes sense for whoever is nearest the top to go first. However, it is probably best to give way to the discourteous rather than have a silly hold-up.

At a hairpin bend (where the inside corner angle is under 90°) and other "tight" corners a carefully timed hoot can be useful to warn an oncoming racing cyclist, who is leaning into your side with his head down, that you are there. But I am afraid it won't work if he has a Walkman on full blast. And it won't make any odds to a gaggle of geese around a corner. They keep coming regardless! So never rely on your horn. Nevertheless accident insurance claim forms usually have a question "Did you sound your horn?" which shows the importance experts attach to the warning a horn can usefully give in a great many different circumstances.

Hairpin bends are very often in steep mountainous country. With such a tight corner slow speed hardly needs emphasis. Downhill, 2nd gear and footbrake control, will be necessary. Uphill, the **Almost Stopping . . . But not Quite** technique of **PART ONE** may come in handy at the apex of the corner if speed is down to a trickle but, if the hill is too steep, you will have to take 1st gear on the move. The change is easy when left to the last moment before the car stops.

Carry it out smartly just like any downward change and "feather in" your re-acceleration afterwards. There is no need to jump on the accelerator and lurch forward. If the change fouls up for any reason, stop. Pull on your handbrake *firmly* and follow with an (up) **Hill Start.**

Ability to take 1st on the move successfully is essential, and not just for country hairpin bends! You can suddenly need it at any uphill point where speed has had to drop to almost nothing, for example, when turning sharply into a steep uphill opening. Find some steep uphills to practise the change aplenty before you get caught unready.

Some hairpins are even worse. Never mind speed having to drop a trickle, you actually have to stop half-way round – and then reverse back (**LOOKING BEHIND!**), before you can get round at all! And if appropriate wait for uphill traffic to get round first . . . See page 100.

On country lanes you need a sharp eye to watch for gates, stiles or anywhere from which people, animals, wild game, etc., may suddenly emerge on foot. You need to be prepared for pedestrians walking on the "wrong" side of the road not just the "right" side (see your Highway Code). You must also watch for tree roots, boulders etc., which may bulge from the edges on sunken roads. Obviously you don't want to hit ones on your own side. But you must keep an eye on the other side too; because drivers coming the other way frequently swing out, apparently more worried about their car being smashed in the ditch than being smashed into you! Don't fall into the same error yourself. See page 95.

Having spoken of distance out, and of watching edges in country lanes, I must stress that one of the most dangerous faults you can acquire is over-concentration on that, to the exclusion of looking ahead where you are going! If you *ever* find yourself driving solely by reference to the edge – LOOK AHEAD AT ONCE. Aligning yourself correctly in the road then comes naturally, without conscious thought.

To return to animals on country lanes (or anywhere else!), you must always be prepared to stop whilst they walk round or pass by. As horse-riding becomes more popular, for example, too few drivers seem to appreciate how volatile a nervous or surprised horse can be. It is far easier to move on again having slowed right down than it is to make a sudden stop should a horse rear up and throw its rider.

FOLLOWING OTHERS

If the driver in front stops suddenly, can you?

There is a long time-lag between the moment the chap in front brakes (or hits something) and your reaction. It is caused by the *THINKING TIME* which you need. His brakes may also be better than yours. The space you leave between you and the vehicle in front must therefore allow for *thinking* and braking time. I will return to this **Gap To Leave** in a moment.

TRAFFIC STOPS

Meanwhile, in traffic hold-ups, if the queue moves only a little at a time, the gap which you leave can fall to as little as 6 metres between pull-ups, closing to under 2 metres when stopped. Leave extra space at uphill stops lest the car in front slips back.

If there is a side turning as you queue on a major road, especially on your left, *do not move up and sit there blocking it off!* Think of the man from opposite you (who isn't necessarily in sight yet) who will want to turn right, into it, or of someone arriving to exit from that road. Why "put a cork in it" for them? See also **More To Watch Out For At Lights** in **PART THREE.**

Normally at each stop, use your handbrake, go out of gear and then release your foot pedals. Adopt the full **Smooth Start** routine with 1st gear for moving on.

If it is obvious you are going to move on virtually *straightaway*, it is permissible instead of going out of gear, to keep your clutch pedal down and take 1st immediately, in readiness for **Key to Fig. 11, 5 of the Smooth Start.** But don't make it a regular habit. If things change and you are going to have to wait, take the gear out and release your clutch. Sitting in gear with the clutch down can be dangerous if your concentration slips. Especially avoid it at places where pedestrians are walking across in front of your bonnet. It also causes unnecessary (and expensive to repair) wear on the clutch thrust mechanism.

For stops of *no more than a few seconds* on **level** road, you can also omit the handbrake, simply holding the car on the footbrake all the time instead. For moving off you omit **Key to Fig. 11, 5** (because your right foot is on the brake). Then, when you come to **Key to Fig. 12, 3,** (b) – having substituted switching your right foot to the accelerator for letting the handbrake off at (a) – you just do a quick juggle as/if necessary to get your feet right for (c) and then **4.** *Short* duration downhill stops can be treated in a similar way. Again however, although missing out the handbrake is allowed if carried out with skill at the right time, it is not a technique to be abused and allowed permanently to displace the proper routine two paragraphs above. When you are the front-marker having to stop at a junction, for example, the examiner will certainly frown if you don't use your handbrake.

You may one day have to stop on a hill so steep you cannot trust the handbrake alone to hold the car. (Or you may have been parked on one.) You know (or your teacher will be telling you!) that your right foot is going to have to remain on the footbrake, holding the car, up to the point of moving, or you will be in trouble. Facing uphill simply combine the above foot-juggle with letting the handbrake off *afterwards*, before your normal **Key to Fig. 12, 3** (c) and then **4.** Facing downhill you just adapt your **Smooth Start Downhill** (near the end of **PART ONE**) by adding in having your footbrake on all the while until you come to let off the handbrake. Then let both brakes off at once and follow by releasing the clutch as explained in that section.

THE GAP TO LEAVE

When you are in a traffic stream and the stream speeds up, you **MUST** increase your *THINKING/braking* gap.

(This is especially so if the long view ahead is hidden, for example, when you have a van immediately in front of you and the road ahead is dead straight. If curves in the road allowed you to see ahead of that van rather better, it might still be safe to remain at your original distance behind it despite a modest increase in speed. However, you would have to be *certain* that the extra vision being gained by looking through past the van, was sufficient to enable you to predict accurately whenever its driver might have to stop. Another time you can occasionally remain closer than might otherwise seem prudent is when a car has exceptionally wide windows which you can see clearly through. Nevertheless, you probably wouldn't stay unusually close like this unless you were looking for an opportunity to overtake.)

Extend your *THINKING/braking* gap for narrow or busy places, blind bends, nearing obstructions, passing through junctions, where there are walkers etc., and indeed wherever potential (and perhaps unseen) danger exists. You are safer a little closer *only* where you can see ahead of the stream *well* **AND** where there are no chances of other trouble coming in your way. When room for manoeuvre is tight and lessened by parked cars, or traffic coming the other way, or both, *slow down*. Lengthen that gap. See READING THE ROAD later in this **PART TWO**. Nose-to-tail driving is a killer. Do not take part.

Adjust your gap as conditions dictate.

Inability correctly to relate speed *and position* – see page 74 – to conditions is the number one failure of Learners, Test-passed ones included.

To the dismay of their teachers they speed on into situations fraught with danger. The idea of positioning so as to lessen that potential threat seems to escape them entirely as well.

In many town streets and similar places, I mean by "speed on", *above, anything exceeding walking speed.* When people moan that speed kills they are being inaccurate. It is too much speed at the wrong time in the wrong part of the road that KILLS.

On a multi-lane carriageway all the same applies. Whenever traffic ahead of you starts to bunch up, hold back. Let your gap grow, until the bunching eases.

According to the Highway Code you need to leave an overall stopping distance or gap in good conditions of 5-plus, car lengths at 30 m.p.h.; at 50 m.p.h. you need 12-plus. Over 50 m.p.h. you need exponentially more.

Another way the Code suggests to judge on dry roads is to leave a 2-second time gap. If you can count slowly to 2 between the driver ahead passing a roadside mark and *you* reaching it, you're about right. My recommendation, to Learners especially, is to make that 3 seconds.

ON WET ROADS because braking is much more tricky LEAVE TWO OR THREE TIMES THE STOPPING SPACE REQUIRED FOR DRY CONDITIONS. REDUCE SPEEDS IN GENERAL BY ONE THIRD OR MORE. For ice and snow refer to SKIDS in **PART FOUR.**

LEAVING ROOM FOR OTHERS TO OVERTAKE

To maintain your stopping room isn't the only reason you should allow those in front to become further away as the stream-speed increases. Unless it is your wish to overtake them, an increasingly long gap is needed so as to allow sufficient space for faster traffic to pass you.

When a stream of selfish drivers, who don't follow the above Highway Code recommendations, forms, faster drivers can only pass at risk to themselves and you. A prime example of this problem occurring is when a long line of cars caught behind a lorry plods along for miles. Of course all must be patient and wait for a safe time to pass. However, if the driver immediately behind the lorry has a slow car or is not prepared to plan to use overtaking opportunities, he really must help by dropping back, allowing others to "leapfrog" him one by one as they pass the lorry. *Such consideration for others is the essence of good driving.*

When you are being overtaken never swing out or accelerate. Indeed, slow down if necessary if the overtaker has to cut in, no matter *what* your feelings may be. (You may not be able to see *why* he's being forced to move in swiftly. You dare not risk being part-cause of a head-on accident. And besides, your own car could be smashed.)

However, use your judgment. If an overtaker has suddenly started to drop back instead of passing, you must keep going, so that he can get in behind you quickly.

EMERGENCY STOPPING FROM HIGH SPEED

Whilst I don't recommend you to drive much over 50 m.p.h. until long after your Test, it is important for you to grasp at an early stage what can happen when you suddenly have to stop from a greater speed.

Get your teacher to demonstrate on a dry day on an empty, safe, dual carriageway (perhaps at first-light), how the distances needed to stop rise out of all proportion once you are up to big speeds. (Any speed above about 40 m.p.h., I call big.) And how downhill, the problems become even more acute.

Imprint what those extra distances look like into your own mind, ready for the day when you may need them. Conjure up in your mind's-eye too, how much worse it can all be in wet conditions with your tyres trying to slither instead of stopping. Study **Skids When Braking Hard** in **PART FOUR.**

SEEING BEYOND THE CAR IN FRONT

Take your cue from the advanced driver and try to avoid following traffic directly in line. As already noted as being a useful tip for dual carriageways, drive, wherever possible, slightly to one side of the "footprint" of the vehicle in front of you, so as to enable you to see round and ahead of it for danger. Notice how the greater you make your *THINKING/ braking* gap, the better your vision out ahead of the vehicle immediately in front becomes, and the *less hidden you will be from oncomers*. A metre or two back makes a dramatic difference. It also gives you the chance to spot cyclists or pedestrians that the man in front, and you, will have to move out to pass.

WARNING PEOPLE BEHIND

Suppose you see looming up a reason for slowing down, or you see the brakelights of a vehicle in front go on. Always react early rather than late. Press your brake pedal lightly or as required. This puts on your own brakelights at once warning anyone behind. If the prospective slowing up is slight (or even unnecessary) you lose nothing, but in an emergency:

(a) you are ready "covering" the brake pedal with your speed in check and

(b) the drivers behind have been warned and

(c) if the road surface is unexpectedly skiddy or your brakes have failed, you will know at once, hopefully early enough to initiate an alternative strategy.

Sometimes you will see the brakelights of a car several places ahead come on, and be able to warn those behind you even before a less alert driver immediately ahead of you has reacted!

In non-emergency stopping make gradualness your byword. Always aim to slacken speed gently, so that you avoid sudden stops. Frequent jamming on of your brakes is a sign that you are not anticipating problems far enough ahead. Take the hint. . .

Once you feel that your brake-power is sound aim to spread your braking across the full distance you have available, less a little safety margin. That way you never brake more than necessary. You always give those behind a fair chance to stop safely too – a policy that will serve you well.

If you are in a traffic stream which is stopping, say at a zebra crossing, you will demonstrate better driving if you can also manage an arm slowing down signal. See page 145. This arm signal carries a bonus of alerting not only pedestrians but also *oncoming* traffic, as well as those behind you. It is especially useful if you are heading the traffic stream. You have to give your signal as soon as you start to slow down. This is because towards your stopping point, when you may need to be changing down the gears ready for moving on again, you will need that arm back in order to be able to keep one hand on the steering wheel at all times. Only give such an arm signal if you have comfortable time. Remember that your priority as you get near to any hazard is to keep *both hands on the wheel*. You might have to swerve. This applies on Test as in everyday driving. No examiner would expect otherwise.

GEARS IN TOWN

Always being in the right gear in the usually heavier traffic of town is quite an art! Re-study fig. 16 and the texts headed **Gear Speeds** and **How To Change Gear.**

If you are in a traffic stream in top on a level road in a built-up 40 m.p.h. restricted area when everyone has to slow to 25 m.p.h., the chances are, I regret to say, that no-one will drop a gear for quick re-acceleration after the reason for slowing down has passed. So, as you cannot accelerate rapidly, it is reasonable to pick up speed gradually without changing down. In circumstances like these 3rd gear can be used from lower speeds where it is yet unnecessary to drop to 2nd, and 2nd can be used from a crawl. However, if you are stream leader in a similar setting, you should avoid such dawdling off the mark when the position opens up. *Change down* for quicker acceleration, and make sure you are never one to frustrate sharper-minded drivers behind. I'm not suggesting you develop habits of speeding in towns, or of ever going faster than safe but do get on with it as you pick up speed again.

If you are slowing down along with all the other traffic but there is a good chance none of you will need to stop, make sure you get down into 2nd gear so that you can pick up smartly as soon as the time comes. Be alert. Stay tuned! On Test you are expected to make normal progress, not dither around when you could be getting on.

It is usual to go up and down your gears in numerical order. However, with the speeds appropriate in or near towns, many drivers skip from 4th to 2nd gear or, maybe, go direct from 3rd to 5th. They regard that as normal. I doubt whether many examiners would be much impressed. Don't let poor habits creep in.

Should traffic drop to a snail's pace but *without stopping*, you can stay in 2nd gear and use your **Almost Stopping . . . But Not Quite** routine learnt on your open space. However, if the snail's pace continues for more than a few seconds, it then becomes more appropriate to take 1st on the move. The technique is discussed in connection with hairpin bends on page 78. You are then ready to slow down even more without actually stopping! You can use the **Minimum Speed – Clutch Pedal Up** technique from your open space practice, initially after the change, and you will still have clutch-slipping in 1st gear in hand before you would have to give up and stop to avoid an engine stall. If all this seems a little esoteric and not worth knowing about, wait till you're in a long hot summer uphill traffic crawl and wish you had taken the trouble to practise! That's when you will save your clutch while others are "burning out" all around . . .

GEARS ON THE OPEN ROAD

Clear of the town you will spend most of your time in top, or in your 5th gear for fuel and noise saving. When you are going over 40 (m.p.h.) 5th is generally fine. However, if you need to boost acceleration from higher speeds, always return to top, or 3rd if more appropriate.

Fig. 37 shows what you must do when you go up and down dale, both for engine braking control downhill and to keep your speed up uphill.

Immediately you start losing speed uphill, take a lower gear and, unless there is a sound traffic reason not to, increase acceleration rapidly to maintain speed. The engine needs more acceleration – more fuel – to carry you up the hill. If the engine "labours" change down at once. (Labouring produces a metallic tinkling noise called "pinking", which your teacher can demonstrate.)

There is nothing worse in conditions where overtaking is impossible, than to have an amateur in front of you who loses every ounce of speed every time you all come to an up hill. (As stopping is easier uphill they can't even claim keeping to a safe speed as a reason for their lack of competence.) Don't join them! Go down as far as 3rd, then 2nd, or even 1st if the hill calls for it, each time dropping gear early rather than late. Return up the gears, of course, directly the hill levels out.

Approaching a steep hill down, you take a lower gear to increase control, and a lower gear still if the hill is steep. At a *very steep hill*, always slow down and take the lowest gear you think you might need, at the top, before you begin the descent proper. You may also need to brake on the way down. 2nd would be the lowest gear normally required.

86

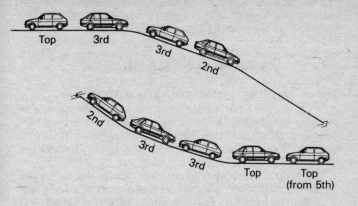

Fig. 37 Using the gears uphill and downhill.

Otherwise you can be faced on the way down with having to change down further, which may be tricky. If you have to do that, you must get speed down with your footbrake to below the maximum of the lower gear before you make the change.

A refinement to your downward gear changing needs mention here. The same road speed in a lower gear needs a higher engine speed. Because of this it is better driving and smoother for passengers if, when you go down the gearbox, you can always try, during that process, to match the engine speed needed in the new lower gear to whatever your road speed happens to be, beforehand. Refer again to fig. 18. During stage **2**, as you are shifting the gear lever, you give a quick blip on your accelerator to raise the engine revs. Continue into stage **3** as normal so that there is no delay. Doing this neatly, so that the revs are a perfect match for your speed as your clutch pedal returns up, soon comes with experience. You learn to adjust the size of blip to the circumstances; the higher your speed is in relation to the new lower gear, the stronger your blip must be.

The technique ought to be within the grasp of most Learners. However, an examiner would not mark it against you if you didn't use it. Nevertheless you will see in SKIDS in **PART FOUR** why a smooth transition down the gears is better driving.

Never, by the way, drive with your hand holding the gear lever. If you have second thoughts about a change take your hand back to the steering wheel till you are ready.

READING THE ROAD

TOWN DRIVING – TRAINING YOUR EYES

In fig. 38, the lines fanning out from **A** represent your eyes scanning for trouble. **K**, immediately in front of themselves, is where most Learners wrongly over-concentrate. Some allow their eyes to wander to the scenery **L**; they will not live long.

You must learn to switch your eyes rapidly about near and far. In the near foreground that means out to the sides as well as right in front of you. Further out ahead always keep an eye on your farthest horizon. Thus, approaching a bend or coming up to the brow of a hill, you watch the unfolding scene *as it opens up*; on the straight you keep searching afar, right to the point where the road fades from view.

Fig. 38, **K**, if there are no pedestrians, is possibly the safest area! You cover that instinctively whilst you absorb the changing traffic situation further ahead.

Your eyes anticipate a door opening from car **B** and someone jumping out onto the road. So you steer a door's width clear, or instead *slow right down* if you haven't room to do that because of oncoming traffic. You stop if necessary. If you saw someone preparing to leap out as you came along you would probably toot your horn in advance but you would allow that it might not be heard by someone deaf.

You take in path **J** to be sure no skateboarder or child cyclist is about to zoom out into the road.

You watch the wagon **D**, which is arriving a little too quickly to turn left and join your road, to be certain it does manage to stop.

E is a wet and therefore slippery patch you may not note till a split-second later.

You have in mind that the Learner driver **C**, going right, has not yet stopped and that he may simply drive out in front of **F**! Is **F** watching **C**? If **F** swung your way in that circumstance, could you give him room even though he ought not to?

Once you have seen the wet patch **E**, you slow down more, wary in case motorcyclist **G** attempts to pass **F**, skids and

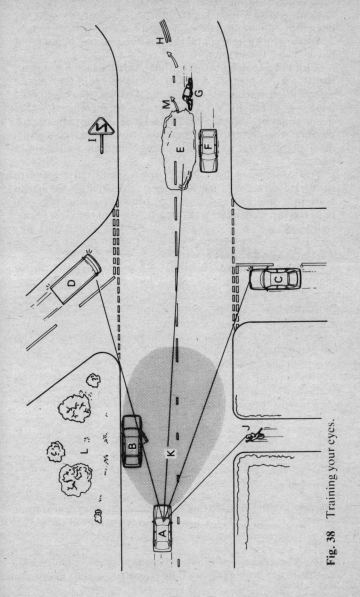

Fig. 38 Training your eyes.

slithers across "your road" towards **D**.

Your glances include **H**, warned by arrows **M**, the beginning of a double white line, and **I**, a double-bend sign.

You are lucky here that there has been no-one behind, but have you been watching?

A lot to be looking for? Yes, but a safe passage lies in your hands, for the *planned avoidance of danger is at the heart of safety*. When a scene closes in fraught with so much potential danger as in fig. 38, *YOU* can slow down; *YOU* can (within the confines of your side of the road and lane discipline) pick the line that offers you the maximum room for sudden manoeuvre; *YOU* can avoid always blaming only the other party.

You can spot a lazy, lousy driver ahead most easily in town. He drives at a constant speed apparently making no allowance whatsoever for what is going on around him. He goes too fast in danger, and often too slow in the clear. Keep well away!

TWO "EXPERT" TIPS

(a) In situations like that in fig. 38 keep a thumb or finger ready at the horn. See fig. 39. A toot can prevent danger – stop a jaywalker for example, or save half-a-second and perhaps a life.

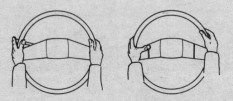

Fig. 39 At the ready to toot, with one finger or a thumb as appropriate, but with both hands still in full control of the wheel.

(b) Also cover your brake particularly, and the clutch too, so that in any emergency no time is going to be lost in moving your feet for stopping. Let your feet "hover" over the pedals as in fig. 40, *without necessarily pressing either one unless you need to do so*. Speed will reduce anyway – because your foot is off the accelerator. If it gets too low your right foot can occasionally switch to give a dab of acceleration, returning to the "cover" position while danger lasts.

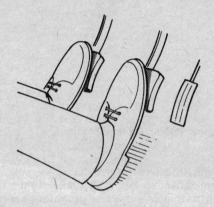

Fig. 40 The "hover cover" position, at the ready for a quick stop.

Suppose, looking at fig. 38 again, that on your approach to the scene some children had been tomfooling near the front of parked car **B**. Perhaps your only clue was tell-tale feet seen under the car at a very early stage. You did look, didn't you? It is when such horrors as those children burst out into your path, forewarned or not, that you will be glad of my two "expert" tips. The U.K. has one of the highest rates of accidents to children in Europe. Let's get it down.

MORE REFINED ROAD READING

In fig. 41, typical of a high street scene in front of you, you have a clear space ahead but traffic in the other direction is queueing. This is no time for wild acceleration or speed.

Here, the van, pulling out between the stopped traffic across a "keep clear" section, nearly went right ahead. Luckily he spotted the motorcycle which had suddenly weaved out to pound up the outside, and he stopped in his

Fig. 41 A time NOT to accelerate wildly.

tracks. Potentially a second later that rider could have been thrown up in the air to land under *your* front wheels. The chances of a jaywalker wandering out through such stopped traffic, or of someone from your left dashing without looking, over to the bus, and of similar errors of judgment are high.

The situation demands single-file use of your side of the road and very modest speed. You will see people trying to barge past, making a second lane and attempting to shoot ahead, to the horror of the stopped traffic so close by. That you cannot prevent. But never join in.

Examine fig. 42 in which you are driver **A**. Apart from checking for jaywalkers like **H** who may leave the pavement thoughtlessly, *especially in rain*, which always seems to cause those on foot to forget their personal safety, you need to glance at the oncoming vehicles. **E** in particular may, not noticing your L-plate, decide to pass **D**, forcing you to use some of your *safety margin* **K** between you and the pavement, or to brake. Watching his front wheels – *without dwelling on them* – is one way you can anticipate his wrongdoing for, unless a car is skidding, it follows its front wheel direction.

Many roads occasionally narrow down without much warning. It is a dangerous error to let yourself be forced out suddenly, as indicated by the dotted line in fig. 43. You can even find yourself having to pull up as the dotted outline car

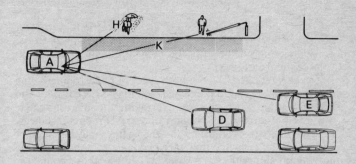

Fig. 42 More refined eye-flashing.

has, whilst better-positioned traffic passes by. That would be a matter of **Lane Discipline** which we come to shortly. Meanwhile the solid arrow shows how the more refined road reader spots the problem way ahead and eases out smoothly to avoid being squeezed.

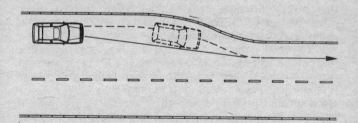

Fig. 43 Road narrows. Ease out early as continuous arrow shows.

PEDESTRIANS CROSSING

Wherever a pedestrian chooses to cross the road he has *right of way*. He may be utterly foolish but you cannot wilfully hit him. As a driver you are duty bound to take the best evasive action you can. In that sense he *must have* universal right of way.

So it is not only at a Zebra or Pelican crossing that you must assume the pedestrian is king; you must be watching everywhere.

Zebra and Pelican crossings give pedestrians particular priority. They are illustrated/described in the Highway Code. At Zebras roadside beacons flash day-and-night to make sure you see them early.

Zigzag lines either side of both types of pedestrian crossing define the area around it in which you may NEVER park and where, on the approach side, overtaking the nearest vehicle towards the crossing is banned under ANY circumstances. Assume the bans even where the zigzag lines may be faded or absent. Whether, when there are two lanes, we should define moving up alongside as "overtaking" in the above context is unclear in the Highway Code. However, I wouldn't push your luck, whether there are pedestrians you are both stopping for, or not.

At a Zebra, if people are still standing on the pavement, you don't have to stop. *But you must be ready to do so*.

Once anyone has stepped onto the crossing, then, even if they are still waiting, you must stop unless too sudden a stop risks a pile-up from behind. Otherwise if you drive where they are about to walk, *you are at fault*.

Should someone rush across quite without warning – so that you have no chance to go through safely – then you *must*, of course, EMERGENCY STOP TO SAFEGUARD LIFE even at risk of a hit from behind.

For normal stopping at a Zebra it is *better* to stop a little short of the official stop line. Pedestrians will appreciate your care and it helps them to see round and behind you in case someone isn't paying attention and stopping.

Train your eyes to look at both pavements on approach. If anyone is crossing you must stop, or slow sufficiently, using speed judgment and common sense, so that he has passed *well before* you get there.

When you have been the first to have to stop, and the last walker has crossed far enough for you to continue, you go, but not so soon as to frighten him. Never rev your engine to try to hurry him up; never move your gear lever into 1st till he has just passed.

Where there is a centre island in a Zebra crossing each side is treated as a separate crossing. However, as a centre island is not a very safe place to stand and wait, it is best for anyone waiting to cross your half of the Zebra from that middle point, for you to give way anyway, regardless of whether they may have actually stepped off the island.

Pelican crossings differ from Zebras mainly in the way the lights are added to control the actions of drivers and walkers respectively. But remember the pedestrian is *always* king, at fault though he may be! The rules for drivers are set out in Question 6 in **PART FOUR**.

Always err on the side of stopping at Zebras and Pelicans if there is *any* doubt that a pedestrian will stick to the rules. However, never wave a pedestrian on, even if he has every right to go. That is unlawful and can be dangerous. It is for the pedestrian to look out. A slowing down arm signal is the only correct one you may give him so that he knows you are stopping. As mentioned earlier give one in good time if you can.

STOP! CHILDREN CROSSING PATROL

When the patrolman steps out displaying his sign you must stop. Apply the same care as for a Zebra. Policemen or traffic wardens often do the job too. Be sure you fully understand from the Highway Code the authorised signals that they use.

GIVING WAY

As far as possible let ambulances, fire engines and police cars pass when you hear their sirens or see their flashing lights.

OBSTRUCTIONS – PASSING PARKED VEHICLES

When passing any obstacle on your side of the road the *rule of the road* is that if there is no room because of approaching traffic you *must give way*.

You slow right down and if necessary wait till you can pass safely *without any approaching vehicle having to decelerate, brake, or – worse – take avoiding action*. The test is, will the oncomer have to slow or move over? If so, or if doubtful, GIVE WAY.

Nevertheless, if someone is approaching you *uphill* with a blockage on their side, it is courteous if you are able to wait for them instead.

In fig. 44, U wait for approaching cars **A** and **B** to pass. Should a fool or a cad in the opposite situation, when you are driver **A**, misjudge getting round the tree and force you to brake, don't accelerate or swing out in hostility – as too many drivers do. *Slow up*. Two dead cads do not make a gentleman.

Fig. 44 Giving way at a fallen tree.

Treat roadworks similarly. Signs usually alert you before you arrive. Always wait well back and well tucked in to your left, if you have to, so that the largest of lorries could get through the other way should one turn up before you can go. Likewise wait well back if temporary traffic lights stop you (learn the lights' sequence from your Highway Code) or if a workman instructs you to wait.

In fig. 45 you are **A** and need to move out to pass parked car **D**. Mirrors' watching shows car **B** close behind. You think **B** wants to pass. He may not have yet seen **D** if your car hides his view.

Imagine your speed is 35 m.p.h. Because of **B** you give a brief right indicator signal from **1** till your mirrors show **B** realises you are moving out. Cancel it by **2** if no one is coming the other way (or you may find yourself like the car in fig. 47!). You make it brief to prevent **B** or anyone else thinking you are going to turn at **Y**.

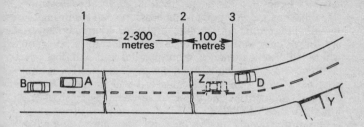

Fig. 45 Passing a parked vehicle.

If no vehicles are close behind *and* no one is coming there is no need to signal.

However, if someone *is* coming, or you cannot yet be sure that there isn't anyone, *do* signal, and maintain that signal as you slow down and assess the situation.

From **1**, in fig. 45, having signalled extra early if there is a **B** on your tail, begin easing out gradually so that by **2** your righthand wheels are running parallel with and just inside the centre line on your own side. You are already in position by **2**, to see past **D** and to decide whether you will have time to go or will have to pull up and wait at **Z**. Learners often leave moving out *too late* and eventually have to stop hard up behind **D**, unable to see round, and being passed and hooted. Ease out early, gradually – never suddenly.

At 35 m.p.h. point **1** would be 300–400 metres from the parked car. Always drop speed by **2** ready for stopping at **Z** if necessary. Between **1** and **2** you take 3rd gear or if need be 2nd. The decision at **2**, whether you will have to wait at **Z**, depends on the traffic conditions; however, if you decide stopping will be necessary, then you must make **Z** fully on your own side and *far back* enough from **D**, for you to be able to see ahead properly whilst you are waiting, and to do so from within your own side of the road.

As soon as you can see you are clear to go on, cancel your signal if you have needed to give one. However, if you are not clear, keep the indicator on whilst you pull up at **Z**. Then it warns people something unusual is happening – i.e. you are stopping. Only cancel it when you set off.

In either event you make sure your signal is off by the time you pass the car – or the first of a row of vehicles if there are several. Even if there is no road **Y** as in this example, signalling beyond that point is unnecessary, and confusing.

Early *positioning* is vital on several more counts. Followers are forewarned well ahead. Oncomers see you sooner. You will be able to pass the car more parallel to it with less of a "detour". (A great swing round the car could well mean that your car would then be off-balance if you suddenly had to brake. That could be the cause of an unnecessary skid. See SKIDS in **PART FOUR**.)

Quite often being nicely "lined up" also allows you to go on safely at times where, because of someone coming the other way, you otherwise could not consider it. This is because road widths frequently turn out to be such that, when the oncomer has been able to see you early and it has been safe for him courteously to move in to his left a little to help, and he has done so voluntarily, there is *then* room for everyone and you are ready to make use of it.

However, you should beware any risk of becoming the meat in a sandwich! In fig. 46 you are **A**. There seems to be plenty room to pass the parked vehicles without crossing the centre line but **E** is coming fast, overtaking the other traffic. Should you go through? The answer in all similar situations is never to go on where there is the slightest chance you might be squashed. Car **E** could be forced out by **F**. (Car **F** may not have seen **E** in his mirrors, and may suddenly swing out – as shown dotted – if **D** opens his door.) A pedestrian might step out from between the parked vehicles on your side or a driver jump down from his cab. One of the parked commercial vehicles could pull out on its way without warning.

Slow down in advance of the sandwich situation and time it till **E** has gone. Stop if you have to, although, once your anticipation and judgment of speed becomes good, stops are often avoidable.

E shouldn't be trying to pass when you are coming, and he should *always pull back* rather than attempting to swerve past **F** should **F** stray out. However, if you were too close to the centre line or going too fast you would be at fault too. Guilty because you had left yourself no room for errors, albeit other people's, but ones which are so common they *must be expected*.

Remember my pleas that you switch your eyes rapidly everywhere, look far enough ahead, and *plan* to avoid danger. If you follow them without fail and always drop

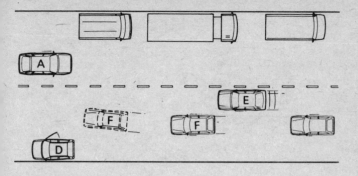

Fig. 46 Meat in a sandwich.

speed, and position accordingly, then untimely actions by others ought never to catch you off guard. You will always have taken the optimum line for a safe passage, invariably have speed sensibly in check ready, and rarely, if ever, find yourself without a safe margin of room for sudden manoeuvre.

See fig. 47. If like this driver, who has no thought of turning, your indicator still flashes away merrily long after some previous use, cancel it. Others may try to tell you it is happening by a seemingly unnecessary toot or a headlight flash but the warning light and ticking sound inside your car should tell you as well!

PASSING CYCLISTS AND ANIMALS

Leave cyclists extra room (1½ metres plus) even if it means slowing and tagging *well behind* for *several hundred metres* before you can pass. Cyclists frequently wobble to get around such atrocities as unmarked pot-holes; or a buckled wheel pitches them off altogether. Make due allowance for age when you come across children on bikes.

If you reach an obstruction, or a junction where you are about to turn left, at the same time as a cyclist, always let him go first. You dare not risk squashing him. He may well swing unexpectedly widely round the roadworks or whatever; he may not be turning at the junction . . .

Leave even more room and take more care when you need

99

Fig. 47 If your indicator has failed to return to normal by itself, cancel it! Here, someone might conclude you were going to turn into the driveway or the lane.

to pass animals. Their unpredictability demands it.

Always signal these passes in advance even if on a wide road you won't be moving out much. This alerts people ahead or behind that there is a problem they may not yet have noticed or be able to see. At night, when vision is hard anyway, particularly out in the country, your signal may be crucial to safety. On the subject of cyclists, these vulnerable venerable creatures can also benefit from your commonsense help when they move to a crown-of-the-road position for turning right. If you can just hold *extra* well back or keep *extra* well to their left, other road users from every angle of view will have a greater chance of seeing them in good time and keeping clear themselves.

SINGLE TRACK ROADS WITH PASSING PLACES

Glaringly obvious examples of these are invariably sign-posted. Where you must take extra care and follow the same basic rules is at *unmarked* narrow places!

The general rule is that traffic going uphill has priority; if you are going downhill you should wait in a passing place – or just opposite one – so as to let the uphill driver(s) pass by. However, there is little point in someone (or several people) coming down, having to reverse a huge distance uphill when you are coming up, if the nearest passing place is much nearer for you to drop back to. Apply sense! Unfortunately you cannot force others to do so but they usually do. Naturally, you should never park in a passing place whether so marked or not.

At the point of squeezing past you may be better as a Learner, to do the waiting, so that the oncoming driver runs the risk of touching your paintwork rather than the other way round.

These rules should be applied much in the same way in narrow residential or commercial streets where cars, skips, etc., are parked all the way down both sides, leaving only one vehicle width down the middle. You all have to treat occasional parking spaces (of which there are bound to be some) as the passing places, and act accordingly.

Narrow bridges, over or under, at which opposing traffic cannot pass are often found on otherwise reasonable width roads. They need similar commonsense treatment. Even if signs allow you priority always be prepared to wait for oncoming traffic which still comes through. Don't go a bridge too far!

LANE DISCIPLINE

With 2 or more lanes for traffic in your direction you may need to move to another one prior to making a turn, or perhaps in order to overtake. Another reason for wanting to move can be that your own lane "fizzles out". Perhaps you are in an outside lane when someone ahead is having to slow and then wait before turning right. Perhaps, as can happen to any lane, roadworks intervene. A parked car may mean you have to leave a lefthand lane temporarily. It all requires constant anticipation, and that means looking a surprisingly (to Learners) *long way ahead*.

Whatever the reason for doing so may be, you cannot just barge across into a lane next door to yours if that one is full of flowing traffic. None of them should ever be placed at risk or forced to slow down because of you.

The rule is that you have to **GIVE WAY** *and let that traffic flow on.*

You wait your turn before you join it. That will probably at least mean having to slow down. Ultimately it can mean having to stop. How it turns out will depend upon when a safe gap to merge into that flow becomes available. Your anticipation has to be good enough to allow time to signal your lane change and, depending on the circumstances, perhaps for others to "accept" that signal too, before you can

101

go.

So often it is only the very advanced drivers, who genuinely look far enough ahead, who manage to re-align themselves in time, easing across into the necessary lane without affecting anyone else, long before a turn or a blockage is reached. For the rest the turn is upon them, or double (or more) queues are already forming because of whatever the problem is, before they can do so.

If there is suddenly a whole queue having to give way to an adjacent flowing lane, as is all too common when a lane becomes temporarily blocked, each member of that queue must then wait, in turn if necessary. (That is, unless the obstacle clears, in which event they can probably promptly revert to continuing in their original lane.)

Double and even treble or more queues, of course form near traffic lights, roundabouts and other junctions all the time. Here, you must always choose and move to an appropriate queue for your direction *early*. Otherwise you can find yourself "pinned" in the wrong lane unable to get across to the right one. You may then have to pass by a turn or go in a wrong direction. This is because (even if it were safe) you should *not* – in an attempt to swap lanes – selfishly cause an unnecessary blockage to those behind who are correctly laned for where they want to go.

You must stick to a correct lane for your direction once you are in one. The Highway Code specifically bans cutting from one queue to another in order to jump traffic. However, cyclists and motorcyclists *do* weave in and out of crawling traffic streams. You are best to yield. This involves good mirrors' watching and, at first, advice from an alert teacher.

Whenever you change lane, as well as double-checking your mirrors, you ought to give a brief indicator signal beforehand. Follow with a final check flash-look over the appropriate shoulder. No more than the corner of your eye can be enough to save you from a mirror-hopper on either side. See page 77.

Cancel the signal directly you start moving over, unless it needs to continue prior to a turn you are making. (As you rarely need more than half-a-dozen flashes for a simple lane change, it is worth while developing a habit of holding the control stalk on, and then "flicking" it back off again against its spring loading once you have moved over – without letting go in between. Then you can't forget to cancel it!) Although

102

you should always signal before moving to an outer lane or crossing to an inner one, you need not normally apply this rule when you are simply moving back to the left after overtaking, or after passing a parked vehicle. This is so even though "technically" you are changing lanes. However, it is often useful to do so after overtaking on a multi-lane carriageway – see pages 111 and 113 – or on a motorway.

Where a dual carriageway reverts to a single one there is often a bottle-neck with queues forming. Generally the above rules work accordingly, depending on which lane fizzles out. However, because of possible fast-moving traffic shortly to be encountered in the other direction, it is customary – and sane – to let outer lane drivers back in even if it is their lane that peters out.

OVERTAKING

I will deal with single carriageway *single-lane* roads first.

The secret of safe overtaking of anyone driving along ahead of you on such a road lies in staying sufficiently *well back* from that person while you plan the pass. You have to learn with experience how close to him still allows optimum vision but you can be certain that to get cramped up in behind will be folly. From there, easing out for a peep ahead becomes Russian Roulette. From further back it is comparatively safe to move out a fraction for the best view, always at-the-ready of course, to pull back for traffic going by the other way. And it is easier to take advantage of curves in the road to see ahead.

Once clear, assuming no-one following is about to pass you, you signal with your right indicator, take a final check behind flash-look over your right shoulder with the corner of your eye, and then move on out for your overtake, gradually, never in a swerve, accelerating rapidly as you do so.

Remember that if someone is already passing *you* the *rule of the road is to* **GIVE WAY**. *Let them go first.* (It stems from **Lane Discipline** in the previous section.)

Staying further back for best vision delivers another vital bonus. It enables you to begin building up the maximum appropriate acceleration *early*, so that you will be exposed to danger on the wrong side of the road for the least possible time. Remember you have no "rights" out there. You may only use it if it is free.

Very often you will be able to time things so that you will

be in the right gear to accelerate further and have all systems on "go", from the moment a gap opens up for you as the last vehicle passes by the other way. But don't overdo your pre-build-up of speed. You still need to be able to drop back in if a problem appears at the last moment. The above being said, if you never plan your passes on our crowded roads, it is likely you will find yourself forever adding to those awful trailing-along traffic jams we see most painfully behind caravans in the summer.

It is suicidal to take a moment longer than necessary to overhaul whatever you are passing. If you do you can be sure some unexpected disaster will turn up. Whatever it is you are overtaking you need to be going a good 15–20 m.p.h. faster as you pull past, and to have plenty more acceleration in reserve. Never try to pass if you can only do so by going "flat out"; having no spare margin is a sure road to death. Passing long lorries needs superior judgment of pace and even more speed in reserve.

To be sure maximum acceleration *will be available*, if you are to overtake a vehicle doing less than around 45–50 m.p.h. *you must use low gear*. It is usually wise not to change up again until after the pass, in case you "miss" the upward change and lose speed sorting that out. Choosing the right initial gear is therefore important:

   (a) Starting to overtake from below 20 m.p.h. use 2nd.
   (b) Otherwise, from anywhere below about 50 m.p.h., use 3rd.
   (c) If speed is still higher and you are in 5th, always come back at least to top (or 3rd if more appropriate).

VISION and "timing" are further keys. In fig. 48 you are doing a little over 40 m.p.h. ready to overtake the van, and he about 30 m.p.h. Your checks have shown nothing is trying to overtake you. You are signalling. You have begun your gradual moving out. Your acceleration is well under way, correctly in 3rd gear. Space **Y** to your left is available to drop back into should a fast car approach. You can now see well beyond the van. You are still at the stage of judging whether there will be time and room to pass and to return fully to your side safely.

Not only do you have several m.p.h. ready "in hand" for achieving your objective of dispatching the pass in the minimum time, you have maximum acceleration at your toe. But you are not yet committed. You can still switch to a left signal, drop off speed and pull back into **Y** in a trice,

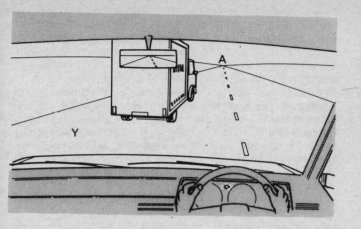

Fig. 48 Overtaking.

probably without even needing to touch your brakes.

For many thousands of miles and many overtakes you will need to be guided at this point by your teacher as to whether to go on or pull back. (Occasionally you may just stay ready for a short distance before deciding one way or t'other but it's not a safe place to hang around long!) He must help you assess whether you have sufficient speed and acceleration available. It may still be safe, for example, despite oncoming traffic already appearing in the far distance. That would depend on the speed of that traffic. Or it could have become unsafe, perhaps because you are now too close to the brow of a hill, unable to see beyond it.

As far as approaching traffic is concerned, the test here is – will they have to slow down, even slightly? If the answer could be "yes", don't go. To be the cause of evasive action is dangerous.

The assessment of whether you are safe to go is usually much harder at night. And it's bedevilled by the assortment of illegal lights one can meet coming, e.g. cars with one headlamp missing! Extend your experience with extreme caution. It is better to wait till you have become fully comfortable with daytime overtaking.

Once you decide, rattle on and GO if your decision is

"yes", or pull back straightaway if it is "no". Avoid half measures. Hesitation, you will have heard, can be deadly.

Nevertheless from your fig. 48 position things can still go wrong. There can still be times when it is safer to cancel the operation *after* committing yourself, than to try to pull it off, risking lives all round. Your teacher must be alert to advise or confirm such changes of plan; he dare not abandon you to hesitation. For example, the van driver may swing out and squeeze you if his concentration lapses – unusual yes, but it happens. He may do it because of a cyclist or child running out on his inside and not seen by you. So, as your eyes continue to scan ahead for danger, also flash them to his front road-wheel. If that doesn't turn outwards, he can't hit you.

Such possibilities make an *advisory* warning hoot *before passing* very wise, especially where roads are narrow and you will have to be closer alongside than ideally you would like.

Normally, you should allow a good bit more than a door's opening width between you and whatever you are passing.

GET BACK TO SAFETY

Though you must avoid "cutting in" after passing, you MUST return to your side promptly. *Do not stay on the wrong side of the road just because it is clear. Get back!* A quick glance in your mirrors, or – much better – over your left shoulder, tells you how soon you are clear to come in. At first ask your teacher to guide you as well. It is nearly always safe far earlier than you expect. So proper looking is vital. Provided the man you pass doesn't have to slow down you can get in as early as you like!

Do.

Finally, check that your right indicator did cancel. It ought to have done so automatically as you moved back in.

Let's suppose that, despite all this instruction, you still make a mis-judgment one day. We all do sometime. You are almost past someone, getting rather too close to the next corner but already *too late to drop back*, when an oncoming car appears around that corner at breakneck speed. Indicate left at once. (You could have had a finger at the ready to do so, knowing you had run things a little tight . . .) This immediately warns the driver you are passing that you are going to be forced to cut in fiercely. And it tells the oncomer exactly where you are going to get out of his way. Simultaneously, GET IN, as fast as you can.

Don't be afraid of cutting in quite savagely. In the split-second this sort of emergency can arise, if the man you are passing is awake – which he should be if you hooted – he will drop back out of your way anyway. Believe me, your greatest crash risk will not be touching his front wing with your back one. Even if that happens it will be better than obliteration through hitting that breakneck oncoming idiot who, incidentally, cannot possibly have been following the Highway Code dictum given on my page 69. Can he?

THE WARNING HOOT

Make your advisory hoot when you can be heard but still have time to drop back. Some "thou shalt not pass" types swing out when they hear you! Perhaps – to be kinder – they hope to warn you of danger ahead, though it is a dangerous way to try to do so. Always hoot weavers. If passing two or more vehicles one after the other, hoot each one in turn. There are plenty around who forget to signal, or forget to check that no-one is passing them, before themselves pulling out to overtake. Nevertheless, remain aware that some drivers are deaf, or deafened by their radio . . .

3 "OVERTAKING" QUESTIONS

1. Is there a *gap ahead* for me to return to? In fig. 48 the van is not close behind and hiding anyone (close-up driving which happens all too often). It is therefore safe. To overtake in nose-to-tail traffic, without the safe-refuge of a gap ahead is criminally dangerous.

2. Even beyond the point of commitment could I still hope to brake in behind the van if necessary? If a driver following you is moving up to block your safety margin – **Y**, fig. 48 – that may not be so. Many evil or stupid drivers do this. If you see that happening, then unless there is absolutely no doubt all is clear ahead, it is better to slow and drop back to safety. Let the fool pass you before you try again.

3. Are *none* of the "DO NOT OVERTAKE" rules listed in the Highway Code going to be broken? Check now that you know them all. If any of those commands would be breached, *wait* for a safer opportunity.

Amongst them for example, the Code urges you *not to overtake* at, or approaching, *any* type of junction. Discipline yourself. Be it a road or just a lane, on either side, that carries a threat to your safety, hold back. It could be your (un)lucky day. That the man in front may be slowing down to turn left is not an excuse. His vehicle may mask something you cannot (yet) see. Never try to pass in this world by risking passing into the next.

On the latter score I come to the question of what to do *whenever* someone is overtaking *towards you* on a single-lane carriageway. If he has plenty of time, fine.

But you MUST REACT INSTANTLY to any chance, *however remote*, that he may not regain the safety of his own side in good time.

Ease off your accelerator, cover your brake, reassess.

That way, if he has made a horrendous misjudgment, you should still stand a chance of stopping or steering out of his way.

The key to staying alive is that instant reaction which allows you to get *your* speed under control. Without it you may be a no-hoper before you know it. Blame him if you will; but blame yourself more for not protecting him.

I turn for a moment to single carriageways which have *more than one lane* each way. They may have occasional KEEP LEFT bollards in the middle but there is no continuous central barrier separating opposing traffic as on a full dual carriageway.

Conjure up in your mind a common situation on such roads, where you are in the righthand lane of two, flowing past slower traffic in the inner lane. It is easy to forget, momentarily, that in reality you are overtaking those slower vehicles rather than merely keeping up with faster outer-lane traffic. It follows from such lapses of concentration that you will inevitably find yourself overtaking at some of the places at which overtaking is banned in the Highway Code, unless you are very fastidious about holding back when you should, and/or getting ahead in good time if that is more appropriate. The most obvious examples are junctions where side roads join. Look in your Code for all the other possibilities. If you carry on regardless, forcing the squeezing of two lanes through such places, *you are in the wrong*. You may feel you are in good company with the majority (who do do such things) but that is no excuse for dangerous driving.

DOUBLE WHITE LINES

These ban overtaking at hazardous places. If you cross a line which you shouldn't, you are breaking the law. If the line is *continuous* your side, don't ride on or cross it. You would only cross to avoid an accident or pass an obstruction or in emergency.

Fig. 49 shows an arrangement of double white lines often found. Two lanes are given to traffic in one direction, only one for the other. This would typically be on a long hill, to enable cars to pass slow lorries etc. in the uphill direction. Don't be lulled into thinking no one will come out of the single lane when you are in the outer, overtaking, lane of the two-lane side. Sometimes the *single lane* has a broken line on *its* side entitling drivers to come out if safe . . .

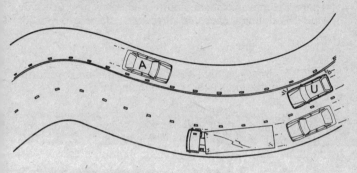

Fig. 49.   A double white line with a false impression of safety.

In fig. 49, **U** would be safe in the outer lane only if you could see all was clear through behind **A** well beyond the next bend(s).

OVERTAKING ON 3-LANE 2-WAY ROADS

Traffic on these roads frequently drives faster than on ordinary single carriageways. Often three lanes are not actually marked; there is a single dividing line in the middle but the width of the road and the weight of the traffic makes 3-lane usage the accepted norm for that particular road.

Custom and commonsense largely dictate the practical rules for overtaking in the middle (laned or unlaned) of these perilous highways. The Highway Code merely contents itself with saying that you have no more right to use the middle lane than a driver coming from the opposite direction.

You **ALWAYS** *give way* to an approaching car *already in the middle*. (And, if I may remind you, to one there from behind!) For example, in fig. 50, **K** is contemplating passing **J** but **A** is already *in the middle lane*, here half a mile distant. It is difficult to show the full distance within the perspective of a small line drawing, so I must ask you to imagine **A** is further away than I can draw him. If you were **K** you might imagine, "I will be safe to move to the middle lane and pass because **A** can drop into the gap between **C** and **D** before I get through." *Don't do it.* Let **A** come on. He may wish to keep in the overtaking lane to pass **D** and **E** and **F**, especially if the road is clear behind you.

There are more reasons. Courtesy is one. Others include the fact that your stream ahead has no safe-refuge gap for

Fig. 50 3-lane, 2-ways.

you to drop into; the only way to get in might be to "force the issue" which could leave you in danger if one of the drivers was nasty. C might close up on D and leave A similarly caught. Or, A's gap could shrink anyway because of F having to slow down rapidly due to some cause now behind you and possibly therefore unknown to you.

The result if both you and A were left high-and-dry in the middle lane would be a potential disaster. You and A would both need to brake hard but there might not be enough time to avoid a crash. The fierce braking might throw either of you into your respective opposing line of traffic. There might be a car Z following close on A, *but unseen by you* till A had filled the gap C–D. By the time you had realised he was coming too, or vice versa, it could be too late for either of you to take avoiding action. A may not be overtaking. He may be stopping – ready to turn right into the gateway . . .

When you are in the middle, yourself overtaking, you must be prepared for someone coming the other way to pull out into your path regardless of custom or sense. Therefore, whilst in the middle, you must *always* have a "bolt-hole" safe-refuge gap in mind; otherwise don't enter into, or stay, in the middle.

If you are going to overtake more than one vehicle, keep your right indicator flashing all the time. Switch to the left indicator briefly when you are about to move in. During daylight overtaking of this sort many drivers add dipped headlamps, keeping them on all the while that they are in the middle lane. It is wise because it draws oncoming drivers' attention to what is happening.

By using speed judgment you can often avoid the situation in fig. 51. W is passing X at the precise second Y goes the other way. For a moment he becomes the meat in the sandwich. The slightest miscalculation by anyone could be disastrous, as might be a mechanical fault, burst tyre etc.

Faced with possible though not actual danger like this, choose the lesser risk. Thus W would stay nearer to X than to Y, because hitting X would be safer than a head-on crash with Y. Y should keep closer to his edge than to W. This is defensive driving, the importance of which is scarcely realised. If more cars are close behind Y, W's risk is greatly increased, as any one of them may pull out.

All this is taking refinement too far, you may feel, but it's precisely these finer points of driving that distinguish the

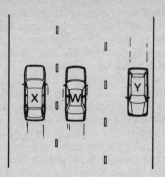

Fig. 51 3-lane, 2-way, passing technique.

master I expect you to be, from the amateurs who are everywhere.

Room For Me Too?

Never blindly follow another driver who is also overtaking in the middle, in the hope that "somehow" there will always be room for both of you to return to your own side. If he is suddenly forced to brake to get back in, where do you go? Once more you must be certain of your own safe-refuge bolt-hole gap, and that it is not suddenly going to turn into his! You've got to be looking far enough ahead too, to *know* that the whole (double) stream in your direction is not about to come to a forced halt. Nothing shrinks your safe-refuge gap faster or deposits you at the pearly gates quicker.

DUAL CARRIAGEWAY OVERTAKING

The last point above has its relevance on dual carriageways too.

If you are driving too fast, and too busy eyeing whatever you are passing to notice that traffic ahead is crunching to a stop, you may find yourself joining that crunch.

There is no substitute for watching that the traffic ahead is moving all the way to the horizon. If that horizon telescopes down because of a blind bend or going up over a brow, hold back.

Whatever anyone else may be doing, **YOU** *have got to be*

112

able to stop if, when you get round that corner or over that brow, you are suddenly faced with stopped traffic or a crash.

You *must remember* your **Lane Discipline** and use your mirrors carefully on duals. No pulling out whilst others are ready to flow past. **WATCH OVER AN AMPLE PERIOD OF TIME TO BE SURE NO ONE IS THERE**. Take a last-second glance over your right shoulder to be *certain*.

If you plan to move out to a middle lane of 3 beware of someone thundering up past you in the *outside* lane who chooses that same moment to return to the middle lane. It's a common crash scenario.

If you are overtaking several vehicles before returning to the left lane (or to the middle and then to the left lane) of a dual or multi-lane carriageway, cancel your right indicator once you are beginning to overhaul them (unless you are intending to move further to your right). It may help others know what stage you intend to move back in if you then give a brief left indicator before so doing.

If it's to a middle lane you are returning initially, look out for an inside-lane man who picks that same time to pull out. Although he ought to GIVE WAY to let you come in, you don't want to slap your sides in the middle. It wouldn't be funny enough for that!

Remember that outer lanes are for overtaking only. Get on with it when you are passing. Nothing irritates more than someone who creeps past whatever they are passing, holding up faster traffic behind, when they could perfectly well have finished long ago.

If you are overtaking a row of considerably slower traffic take very great care that none will pull out on you. (Note: a toot in time is sometimes divine!) Don't imagine that you need not worry so much if you are in the middle lane, on the grounds you could always move out a bit. To swing out like that could put outside lane drivers, travelling faster still than you, into instant peril.

A sudden lurch sideways at high speed could cause you to lose control anyway. Make sure all your lane changes are smooth and gentle.

IN EMERGENCY, ABOVE ALL, YOU MUST STAY IN LANE. Not to, risks that mega pile-up in which everyone prays they will never become involved.

Headlamp Overtaking Customs

On duals (or any multi-lane carriageway) a headlamp flash

113

– seen in your mirrors – has become customary for two different purposes:

1) As a request from a faster driver behind, waiting to overtake, that you move in from an outer lane as soon as possible.

2) As an "all clear" signal from someone you have just overtaken, telling you it is now safe to pull back in, in front of him. These flashes are not included in the Highway Code; indeed the Code attempts to deny their use. Nevertheless they exist. Let them be advisory only. Make certain you are sure it is safe before you move in. Beware the rat who flashes prior to whizzing past on your inside! Or the motorcyclist who weaves through from further behind, unaware of a flash having been given.

PART THREE

JUNCTIONS

WHO GOES FIRST?

A driver is presumed to have a general priority whenever driving forwards on his own side of the road, though this is *not always* the case, as I shall show.

Almost all U.K. roads are classified as being major or minor. You always cede priority to anyone on a major road. At junctions it is usually obvious which is the major road, the minor one having broken lines at right angles across it where it meets the major one. At little-used junctions this may be your only clue. However, more usually, you will find in addition a GIVE WAY sign near its end, together with a large white warning triangle painted on the road. Alternatively, there will be a solid line or lines and a STOP sign. Where equal roads – which I come to last – meet, there are traffic lights to switch the priorities alternately, or we have a roundabout. In the latter case special rules about priority apply.

Police or traffic wardens may intervene at any point of special difficulty, whatever the type of junction.

CORRECT POSITIONING AND RIGHT SPEED

Wherever you meet other traffic or you turn, being in the correct position and having the right speed are the critical factors which save accidents. It is not just the doing it right, that counts for you. It is the fact that your intentions are also thereby made beyond doubt to everyone in the vicinity.

Proper POSITIONING and the correct CONTROL of speed are of greater importance for SAFETY even than signals. *I would rather be driven a million miles by a driver who grasped this fact, than a single mile in "the perfect safe car" with one who had no grip on these cornerstones of safe driving.*

TURNING LEFT

LEFT TURN *OFF* A MAJOR ROAD

In fig. 52 you are going to turn left *off* your (major) road. At **A**, in fig. 52, you are doing 35 m.p.h., some 250 metres from the turn. For clarity I have left out other traffic while we look at the theory.

From **A**, 250 metres out, you double-check your mirrors, put on your left indicator and then start to reduce speed. At **B**, about 175 metres from the turn, you take 3rd gear. By C_1, with about 30 metres to go, braking gently if need be, you should be down to a running pace. Then you take 2nd. You aim to arrive at the turn at *walking pace or less*. With good judgment any braking you need to do will be almost imperceptible. Last-minute fierce braking is bad.

At many tighter turns there will – at least to begin with – have to be a stage shortly before you begin to steer round, where you **Almost Stop . . . But Not Quite** (as learnt in **PART ONE**). This enables you to recapture clutch-slip momentarily, just prior to moving forward again gently, *and under total control*, into the minor road. If the road is steeply downhill as the turning is reached, it may be a case of using the *downhill* **Mile-An-Hour** technique of page 58 instead, just for the final moments before you drive on into the turn.

Otherwise you will arrive too quickly.

You won't have time to steer in properly or straighten up smoothly, and there will be a general panic and danger as you sweep into the turn "on two wheels".

Another Learner's fault to avoid is failing to look ahead along that minor road you are turning into. Is someone about to walk across the neck – to whom you would have to give way if he did? Will you have to wait whilst a wide load exits into the major road? In other words are you still **LOOKING WHERE YOU ARE GOING** despite all you have to think about?

During the whole approach from the moment you first change down, have a continuing eye on your mirrors as ever and hold a steady course well to the left. Pavements are always rounded at turnings so there will be no need to make any outward "detour" before you go round. Just steer round (with rapid steering movements) *at the exact right moment*. This will present no problem provided you are going *slowly enough*. You should be no more than 2–3 tyre widths out

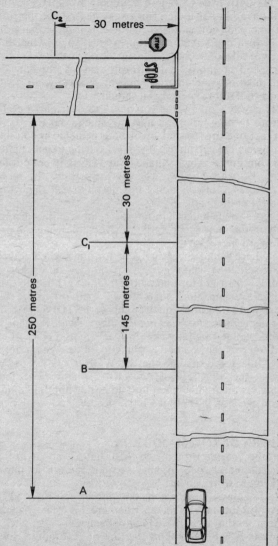

Fig. 52 Making a left turn into a minor road.

117

from the edge as you drive round. But don't get too close either; you will risk sweeping people off the pavement or hitting the kerb itself. Straighten up equally rapidly so that you will have neither under- nor over- steered for the turn, and resume your normal distance out as you re-accelerate in 2nd gear towards C_2, before taking 3rd and so on. Once into your new road don't linger. Get up through the gears to a normal speed promptly, unless traffic reasons prevent you. Resume mirrors' watching straightaway. Cancel your indicator if it has not self-cancelled as it should.

The Highway Code warns you never to overtake a cyclist just before turning left. You have to watch your mirrors as well, in case one tries to slink up on your nearside as you slow down; especially keep an eye if you are having to wait before making your entry. Always make a final check over your left shoulder. Be warned! Two-wheelers, especially the motorised variety, are always doing this despite the danger they run. Wait. Let them go.

On bigger roads a deceleration slip road into the turn lets you pull off the major road earlier; drivers following can pass you safely, sooner. Use it!

Let me here sound a warning gong for times when you are following someone who seems exasperatingly slow when he turns off left (or right for that matter). Don't get up too close to him. Never presume that he will pull off your road completely in one go. Frequently this sort **STOPS**, with the back of his vehicle *still blocking the major road*. Perhaps he has misjudged getting into a gateway. Perhaps a chicken has decided to cross the road he is trying to enter. Why, doesn't matter! Unless you assume that he WON'T GET CLEAR until you see that HE HAS DONE, and hold back accordingly, you are likely to finish up hitting him. Hold onto a gap you can stop in, until it's 100% positive you won't need to.

LEFT TURN *ONTO* A MAJOR ROAD

This time you are on the side road, fig. 52, about to turn left into the major road. Again, I assume there is no one in front of you to worry about.

If the sign says STOP, as in this figure, you *must* **STOP** *completely* at the line, no matter whether all is clear or what a driver in front did, were there to have been one.

Failure to **STOP** = breaking the Law = Test failure. I will deal with what to do if the sign says GIVE WAY a few pages on; for the moment assume it's a STOP sign.

Imagine the distances **A, B** and **C** from the turn along the major road in fig. 52, now applied to the minor road. You double-check your mirrors and then start signalling with your left indicator before beginning to slow down. Reckon to take 3rd as before at **B**, but this time because you will have to stop anyway, you need not go down to 2nd gear. You brake gently, remaining in 3rd, and stop when the front of the car reaches the line. Hold a course well in to the left as before. The same 2 – 3 tyre widths out when you come to the turn itself will be correct. Particularly watch out for pedestrians stepping across the neck as you reach it. They see you slowing up and take it as permission to go! Let them if they do. Take all the same care previously mentioned about cyclists.

To prevent stalling remember to put your clutch down during the final moments.

Once stopped apply the handbrake and slip into neutral before releasing your foot pedals. The handbrake must be on to prevent rolling forward or back. Forward could be deadly; and it is easy to slip back and hit a car behind unwittingly!

You stop with your front bumper *at the line*, not "miles" before, otherwise you won't be able to see properly both ways along the major road. If, after stopping, you still can't see, edge forward until you can and stop again. But, as you do so, be looking to the right, from whence your most immediate danger is likely to come, as well as taking a quick glance to the left to make sure that your car's nose is not going to be chopped off by someone cutting the corner as he turns right off the major road.

For the various reasons noted above, always make your final glide to a stop very gentle. That will give you time to see whether, for example, you will have to stop *before* the line initially, for a walker or whatever. It also gives confidence to anyone coming along the major road that you are in full control for stopping.

When the major road is clear for you, make a **Smooth Start** in 1st gear and go. Remember just before that, to double-check with a flash-look over your left shoulder for any cycle or motorcycle trying to squeeze out between you and the kerb. If you have to wait because of traffic, prepare for that **Smooth Start** by getting into 1st gear just before the last vehicle concerned passes by. Otherwise you will lose count-less opportunities – with someone else always seeming to come up before you are ready. When the right moment comes, keep *well* tucked in as you steer out. Make sure you straighten up so as to reach a normal distance out in one neat operation – all done as you accelerate, without dithering, up the gears to an appropriate speed. Look to your mirrors. Check that your signal self-cancels.

"Clear for you" above, means both that your immediate path into the major road is free – of stopped traffic for example, or pedestrians – and that no one coming from your right will find they have to slow down, even a fraction, because of your coming out. (Pedestrians frequently step out to cross major roads near junctions; indeed, it is surprising how many pedestrian crossings are actually sited far too near to turnings.) A killer you must never fail to check for is *two* vehicles, one overtaking the other, coming from the left. WAIT OR DIE . . .

Looking Right And Left

A common eyeball instruction for emerging at junctions *is look right, left, and right again*, and, *if safe*, go.

But more is needed.

For example, one-ways deceive followers of the above rule. The traffic nearest your bonnet may then whizz past from your left . . .

Not only must you *move your head and neck* (forward or back as needed), as well as your eyes, you must begin looking both ways *well before you reach the line*. Otherwise you won't notice pedestrians stepping off the pavements left or right. They are usually the *first* thing to be looking for. You won't spot corner-cutters in time. See page 119. And your roof pillars will hide danger. Fig. 2 showed the areas they can so easily mask.

Again, if you merely glance too quickly, your eyes will miss joggers and two-wheel riders trailing along the pavement edge from your right. Believe me, never minding them, whole cars can be concealed not only by the roof pillars but also by apparently trivial dirt on your window(s), or on your glasses, or even by your passenger's nose! The human eye remember, has its own blind-spot too.

Take life-loving length looks both ways.

A second look – a sweeping, long enough look – *picks out any moving vehicle previously hidden*. And keep your eyes skinned all around as you set off.

At night, when sideways looks are into darkness, away

from the pool of light from your headlights, GIVE EVEN MORE TIME. Your eyes need it to adjust, before they can see properly the unlit, black-clothed biker, or the dark horse.

Make No Assumptions about anyone signalling left to enter the road you are leaving. See page 148.

In fig. 53 the car driver followed the common eyeball rule as first given above but still crashed. The major road rose more steeply towards the middle than he had anticipated. He had started in 2nd gear when he should have been in 1st. The car had laboured across – almost stalling in the process – and taken longer than he expected.

Fig. 53 "Feeding her" when crossing danger areas.

Had he continued eye-switching right, left and ahead *while crossing*, he would have seen the lorry which had by then appeared, and could have stopped in his own (first) half of the major road. Had he moved more smartly anyway, he would have made it.

The lessons of this story are:

1. Never linger in the wrong gear – you need 1st to cross a major road.

2. Keep eyes "in the back of your head" and all around as you go.

3. Get your accelerator going *resolutely, before, as, and after* you let the clutch up, to be sure to get you over the danger area, safely, quickly. Feed that engine!

Also, the lorry driver in fig. 53 ought to have anticipated that the car might falter. He had a duty to slow earlier – *ready to stop*. Then as the scene unfolded so potentially disastrously he could have pulled up in safety. There were plenty of clues for the observant – the rate the car was moving off, its driver failing to look his way . . ., even knowing that too quick a look by that car driver might not have focused and *seen* . . .

That lorry driver was Part II of the accident.

Being on the major road does not give him, or you, the right to plunder on regardless; it is *not* a licence to kill.

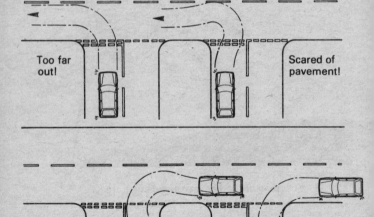

Fig. 54 Bungled "lines" turning left.

Fig. 54 shows bungled "lines" through left turns. You can see them happen every day.

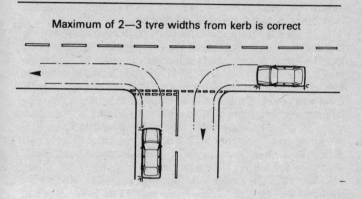

Maximum of 2—3 tyre widths from kerb is correct

Fig. 55 The right "lines" turning left.

Fig. 55 shows the right ways, tucked well in to make the direction you are taking abundantly clear, keeping you well away from other traffic. (If there was an oil spill or black ice there, you might skid; you would be grateful indeed, then, if the space you had gained by taking the proper line saved you from an accident.) Proper positioning at the end of a minor road can also enable a cycle or motorcycle from behind you, who is turning right, (or going straight across if it is a crossroads) to come up alongside unhindered.

See fig. 52 again. If you are turning left onto the major road and the sign says GIVE WAY instead, you *do* take 2nd for the last 20 or 30 metres before your turn. You don't have to stop completely if all is clear. Being in 2nd and at slow speed, you are *prepared to stop or go*, making a last-second decision if appropriate.

If the road-end and the major road are open-to-view, eye-flashing to the right and left (and, if a crossroads, ahead) from well before you arrive – probably further beforehand than usual – enables you to decide what to do:

1. If there is any traffic coming from your right along the major road then, as instructed by the sign, you GIVE WAY. Let them take priority. Unless the traffic is far enough away not to be affected anyway by your pulling out and going left, *stop at the end*. Assuming you do stop, then, after it has all passed, proceed as you would for a STOP sign, meantime remembering handbrake on and gear into neutral.

2. If vehicles from the left are overtaking each other, or there is the remotest chance they might do, again, STOP! Equally, if at a crossroads someone opposite is turning or may be about to turn, right, STOP. (Once he pulls into your half of the road on the way out he becomes, in effect, traffic from your right. Fault would be difficult to prove in court so be prepared to let him go if he is ready to do so.)

3. If, on the other hand, there is no traffic from any direction to affect your turn and no chance of danger to pedestrians, then you can carry on without any stop. Take care (not forgetting your mirrors and a glance added over your left shoulder), and with those eyes ranging. Keep slow so that if a vehicle appears you can easily GIVE WAY at the last moment. Were you not to, and you caused that driver to brake or have to slow down, you would be at fault. Your Test pass could be in doubt. That might depend on whether it was safer still to go, than to try to stop in your tracks.

Having decided to go without a stop, if you do, remember to pick up speed again smartly once you are on the major road. As always, also note the new situation in your mirrors at once, and make sure your signal has stopped flashing.

Remember that early signalling, sensible speed, and taking the correct "line", so that everyone knows exactly the direction you intend to go, is ever-important here – perhaps even more so in the event you don't need to stop.

You must learn to avoid stopping at the line when you don't need to. That creates an unnecessary hold-up. You can also be bumped by someone following you who won't understand why you stopped – who was looking both ways (and seeing them clear) but forgetting to watch you as well. Silly you may think – until you've nearly done it yourself . . . People are entitled to stop at junctions for no better reason than that they haven't looked properly yet. You will yourself at times so why shouldn't others?

LEFT TURNS AT CROSSROADS

I have dealt in no. 2 above with a potential snag as you join a major road at crossroads. In fig. 56, you are **C,** positioned ready to turn left and *leave* one, travelling slowly and within 10–15 metres of your turn.

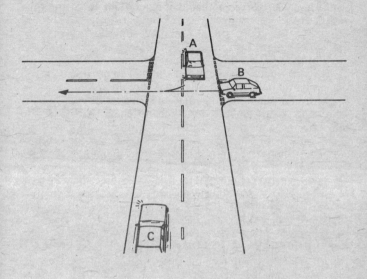

Fig. 56 Crossroads snags.

Assume for the moment there is no car at **A**. Because you are turning left, **B** thinks he can nip across in front and does so. Or perhaps *there is* a right-turner waiting like **A**. He equally, sees you are slowing down to go left, and thinks "I can shoot over first".

Let them go if they start. Reason? It would be more hazardous for them to get stuck having once set off. Because a driver is selfish or foolish or is arguably in the wrong, is no reason for having an accident. Losing your "No-claims" bonus (it is not a "*No* blame" bonus) is costly!

TURNING RIGHT

RIGHT TURN *ONTO* A MAJOR ROAD

In fig. 57 **U** are approaching a GIVE WAY line, preparing to turn right. For simplicity here there is no one else in front of you. You double-check your mirrors, signal, slow down – braking gently if necessary – and drop down the gears just as for turning left (except that it is your right indicator this time!).

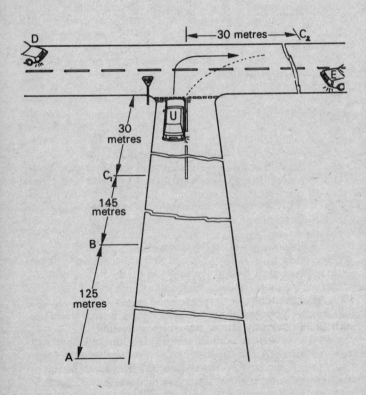

Fig. 57 Right turn onto a major road.

However, it's best to begin everything a little earlier than you would if you were turning left, perhaps 50 metres earlier. This gives you extra time to ease across towards what will be your final right turn position by the time you reach the GIVE WAY lines. (By then the righthand side of your car should be fractionally inside and parallel to the centre line of your minor road at the end – as shown. Visualise that line if none is painted.) Beginning to ease out early makes sure that anyone driving a bit too close behind you swiftly realises you are going to be turning right. It is especially important if you have a choice of two marked lanes at the end anyway, or whenever there is room for two of you to pull up alongside each other when you reach the neck of your minor road. Once you are running just inside the centre line, which you should aim to be by C_1, stick to that. Avoid wandering back to your left.

To return to fig. 57, you would expect to reduce speed from **A**, dropping to about 25 m.p.h. before taking 3rd at **B**, 175 metres from the turn.

If you can see you are going to have to stop (as in fig. 57 because of **D** and **E**), there is no necessity to drop right down to 2nd gear. Pull up in 3rd. Having stopped apply your handbrake and come out of gear (into neutral); be patient till the major road is clear, or about to be clear, both ways.

Once traffic clears from your right (and remains clear), and there is, or soon will be, a safe gap from your left, select 1st gear and bring your clutch pedal up to the biting point; you are then ready to release your handbrake and tail in to that gap. If you are not ready you will miss opportunities. Should traffic reappear from your right before you can go put your clutch pedal down again till it has passed.

If the waiting is now obviously going to be for quite a while again, come out of gear as well for the time being. Begin to prepare once more, as soon as traffic is about to cease both ways appropriately.

If however, there are no problems at the junction itself – such as an obviously unruly bunch of pedestrians – and you can see really well in both directions that all is likely to be clear (sufficiently far to discount the possibility of traffic either way being any problem no matter how fast it comes), then do get yourself down into 2nd gear, by C_1, 30 metres out. Although you keep slowing down ready to stop for an unforeseen change in the circumstances, you are then geared to go ahead and make your turn without a stop.

If you were approaching a STOP sign and line(s) in fig. 57, instead of the GIVE WAY lines, then, as noted under left turns, the law demands that you **STOP** anyway – even if there is no one in sight for miles! Remember that the routine after that (unless the road is level and all is clear immediately) has to be handbrake on and into neutral before you can make a **Smooth Start** in 1st gear once it is safe to go.

The Eyes Have It

Apply everything I said about eyeball-swivelling when making left turns, with equal force on right turns. Don't just look; *focus*. If there is anything coming to be seen, let the eyes have it! Remember to let the corner of your right eye spy over your right shoulder just before you go. If some cheeky rider has crept up alongside on your right, you don't want to knock him off.

Whichever way you are turning out into a major road add this extra precaution. Though looking no less rigorously to all points of danger beforehand and continuing that whilst you emerge, train yourself to be looking in *whichever direction has the least-good view* at the moment of setting off.

Thus, if your view to the right is foreshortened by a thick hedge whilst that to the left is open, be looking right when you go. Then, if anyone speeds into view from there at that critical second, you will be the first to know! You can react with your safest plan instantaneously: whether that will be to stop before you are much out (or even reverse smartly if you are clear to), or press on forward, will depend on exactly how you are placed in relation to that speeding driver – as well as on any evasive action he may be taking. If you dream and look the wrong way as you emerge who knows what may be your fate . . .

And LISTEN too. Open your window(s). There are countless junctions where the view is restricted, at which you can hear (motorised) traffic coming, well before you can see it. That sound can save your life.

Correct "Line" When Turning Right

Don't cut the turn (see dotted line in fig. 57). Follow the continuously-arrowed path, adding speed exactly as you would after coming out to the left, to get you away quickly, safely. Again, watch your mirrors straightaway. Cancel your right indicator if it hasn't already done so itself. Conditions permitting you should be up to 3rd gear by C_2.

Some snags can arise to affect this right turn even when you have taken the perfect theoretical "line". Look again at fig. 57. Car **E** may not slow down enough, and as a result, may do a fast, wide, left-hander, encroaching on your side. Car **D** could do a tight right-hander and "cut off your nose."

The latter fault is common; be prepared.

In either event you may be forced to brake sharply, stop, or move in to your left. The last option would be a last resort, precluded if your mirrors warned of someone already moving up on your inside.

Such a person preparing to turn left would be perfectly correct if there was room. Indeed your proper positioning helps him to do so and this is sensible because, as a right-turner into the major road, you might well need to wait longer than he would have to before being able to turn left into it.

Anticipation has to come to your rescue here. Watch for the possibility of an **E** type rushing in to the turn; hold back and don't ease out towards the centre-line until you are sure he will make it without endangering you. Remember he could skid too. For a potential **D** type, similarly hold back from the GIVE WAY or STOP lines until you see how badly he tries to cut the corner. These menaces illustrate the necessity for starting to look both ways *well before* you reach the line(s) with a major road.

Another possibility to anticipate if the end of your road is narrow, is that of a lorry trying to turn in and needing extra space to do so. Be prepared to hold back and help lorries. They're tough to drive!

Car **D** in fig. 57 can fool you another way as well. If he gives no signal and appears to be going straight on, you may be preparing to tail in behind him, everything else being clear. Just as you start to move he swings right and takes off your front wing! Don't be hasty; watch him!

RIGHT TURN *OFF* A MAJOR ROAD

Study fig. 58. Double-check your mirrors before signalling with your right indicator. Then **U** ease out gradually, beginning 350 metres or more from the turn, to a position running just to the left of the road centre line by C_1, 250 metres from it.

The object is to be in this crown-of-the-road position *before*, or almost before, you need to start to slow down. Now you can change down to 3rd gear and brake a little if

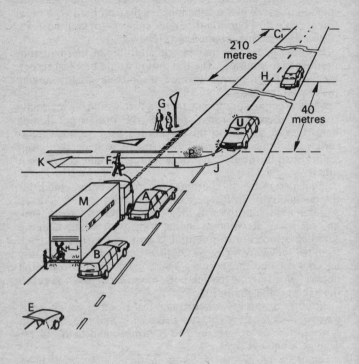

Fig. 58 Right turn off a major road.

necessary, as you carefully judge the speed of your arrival at the turn. Hold that crown-of-the-road position. It tells everyone what you are doing. It lets those behind going straight on begin to filter past to your left as soon as they have room; *otherwise they know they must slow or even stop while you get clear*.

Start signalling earlier if your mirrors are telling you someone is pressing on your tail, so as to forewarn him not to pass. If someone forces past you, you may need to let him go first and even give up trying to turn if necessary, rather than have an accident. However, such dangerous driving is thankfully rare.

You must be in 2nd gear by **H**, in fig. 58 (40 metres from the turn), speed down to little more than a running pace. All the time so far you should have been assessing the oncoming traffic (and taking account of anyone wanting to come out of the turn even though they should wait for you). This is so as to see whether there may be a safe gap in any oncoming stream, for you to turn through in 2nd gear without a stop when you reach the turn (perhaps with a bit of skilful timing and maybe an *Almost Stopping . . . But Not Quite* routine added), or whether you will have to stop where I have showed **U** in fig. 58, and then wait there until you can go safely, using a **Smooth Start** in 1st gear.

Remember the *rule of the road* that traffic **A, B** and **E**, because it is going forward on its own side of the road, has priority. As you will be turning across their path it will be up to you to GIVE WAY and wait if necessary.

If there is a safe gap make your turn without stopping, confidently, but at no more than a fast walk. Unless you are turning into an immediately steep uphill road, in which case you will need to take 1st on the move as explained under **Country Lanes** in **PART TWO**, 2nd gear will supply ample power – always provided you don't teeter to a halt just before committing yourself. Make sure you get into 1st if there is any danger of that.

If you are in *any* doubt that you can cross the path of the nearest oncomer without him having to blink, touch his brakes or make any evasive move, **stop.** Stop with your front bumper sitting above an imaginary line which is an extension of the centre-line of the side road. (I have put the line in, in fig. 58.) Next, put your handbrake on and go into neutral. (However, see **Traffic Stops** in **PART TWO**; you may not need the full handbrake/gear routine.)

Make sure your right indicator is still flashing.

Then, *anticipating* the next safe gap for turning, take 1st gear shortly before the last oncoming vehicle passes. Give resolute (though not ferocious) acceleration before, as and after you release the clutch, to be certain the car will take you safely to **K**, out of danger. Go the instant you can but not without sneaking a glance over your right shoulder in case someone on two wheels has crept up outside of you. You would have to let him go first.

Wait for a gap long enough for you to cross at a mile-an-hour. You go faster but *need that safety margin* in case the engine "coughs" on you, a pedestrian from **F** or **G** wanders into **K**, or anything unforeseen causes you to have to stop at **L**, straddling the oncomer's path. I hope you won't ignore this advice until you have a fright or an accident. If you ever did have the misfortune to find yourself stuck on the way round, anyone coming, like **A**, needs a fighting change to pull up in time. Make sure they would always have it.

The correct "*line*" (long wide arrow) is the same whether you stop or not. You start turning only when the nose of your car passes that imaginary line, *not before*. Never cut through **P**.

In fig. 58, I show the stopping position waiting for cars **A**, **B** and **E** to pass. Don't creep to **J** while waiting for **E**. It prevents a clean turn. When you go, enter the minor road well in to your own side and at your normal distance out, as shown. Capture the new view in your mirrors as you accelerate smartly to an appropriate speed. Check your right indicator has now cancelled.

In the example of fig. 58, I have had to telescope the picture. Imagine how much further back **A**, **B** and **E** would have been at various stages of your arrival from before C_1. During your continuous assessment of whether there might be a safe gap to turn through without a stop when you reach the turn, you may have been unable to judge between C_1 and **H**, or even after **H**, whether you will ultimately arrive in time to turn before **A** is too near. **A** might confound your calculations by trying to be helpful (at his own risk), and decide to slow down or stop to let you through! It is for this sort of reason that you *must always* get down into 2nd gear on your approach. Then you are automatically ready to shift smartly out of danger to **K**, should an opportunity safely to do so present itself unexpectedly.

To be able to reach there under momentum anyway, rather than having had to make a standing start, tends to be safer; a stall can't leave you stranded half way over. But you must always be certain **K** is free for your arrival . . . see below!

Hidden Dangers

Imagine for a moment that in fig. 58, cars **A** and **B** pass by well before **U** arrive to make your turn. **E** is only where he is shown now, not coming fast, and having been much further off prior to your arrival. As it appears safe to do so well before **E** could be inconvenienced, you decide to go on without a stop.

Suddenly, pedestrian **F** turns round and, without looking, strides smartly in front of you across the minor road. **U** stop dead at **L**, heart pounding as you catch your breath. Before you are able to move on, you discover a less obvious reason why the lorry **M** has been so entirely out of order for stopping at the edge where he has. There is a screech of brakes as **E** narrowly manages to pull up without smashing your back wing.

Not only did **M** block the view to the right for drivers who might have come up to exit from the minor road (as well as for drivers like **E** being able to see *them*), he prevented **E** from seeing what was happening to you. Luckily **E** was covering his brake (and clutch) as in fig. 40, and coming at cautious speed, not prepared to chance accelerating before his own view ahead, opened up.

Another hidden danger can be gleaned from fig. 58. When stopped awaiting a gap, **U** should *never* start to turn your steering. If you do and then get hit from behind you will be shunted directly into oncoming traffic. Keep your wheels STRAIGHT till the moment you set off round. This is especially vital on trunk routes with fast traffic, where you may be exposed as the only stopped car.

When your major road is narrower than in fig. 58 a lorry parked like **M** can make it unsafe to move out fully to your crown-of-the-road position early. Hold back a little from your prospective stopping position of fig. 58, until you are sure no oncoming driver will swing out to get round **M**, hitting you in the process. Of course, none should, but people rush and they can be so busy steering clear of **M** that they forget to look ahead – at you!

RIGHT TURNS AT CROSSROADS

At any crossroads imagine a pin, like the beflagged post on a golf green, standing vertically at the point where the centre lines of the two roads would cross. Whichever direction you are making a right turn from, the *basic rule* is: keep this "flag-pole" on your own right. Drive round behind it.

In fig. 59 your path is shown by the solid arrow and those of **A** and **B** by dotted ones. Forgetting who goes first for the moment, you can see that by each of you going round behind the "pin" you will automatically pass the other(s) turning right from opposite, offside-to-offside (with your driver's doors adjacent).

133

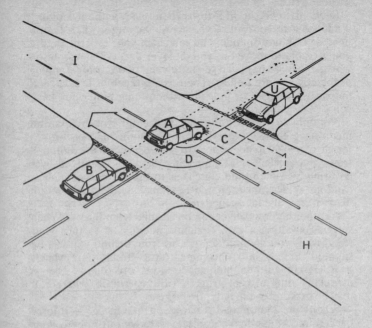

Fig. 59 Right turns at crossroads.

Note: at smaller junctions there sometimes isn't room for this, and the practicalities of space dictate that you need to cross in front of each other nearside-to-nearside. I will deal with these apparently less-regimented junctions shortly, under *Crossing In Front When Turning Right*.

Emerging From The Minor Road

Unless a crossroads which you are approaching from the minor road is obviously clear in all directions, it is nearly always wise until you have gained considerable experience, to stop at the line, come what may. At STOP signs you must anyway by law, but do so at GIVE WAY signs too. Then you will have time to collect your thoughts as well as making certain you will be safe to complete your right turn.

Your mirrors' work, right indicator signal, positioning and

slow approach should be just as already described for any **Right Turn** *Onto* **A Major Road**. *Assuming there is no one waiting opposite to worry about*, you can make your advance preparation to go, in just the same way too (see page 127); and go when clear to do so.

If any major-road driver stops so as to help you, you must still know you are safe from all other directions first – as well as making a check for two-wheelers who may attempt to tear past from behind *him* – before you dare move.

When there is someone waiting opposite however, like **B** in fig. 59, there are further aspects of the *basic rule* to follow.

To help you plan your own actions, begin by trying to establish which way that driver is heading. The way he is positioned will probably be your most reliable clue as to which way he intends to go. An arm signal from him would confirm it but that is rare. Lack of any type of signal may **NOT** mean he wants to go straight ahead, so don't count on that yet. An indicator signal should be confirmation but beware! Those very drivers who leave signals flashing when their use is finished are the same ones who tend to forget to signal; so you can have a driver who flashes one way before going the other!

If, when traffic along the major road (from both **H** and **I** in fig. 59) clears, and if that driver opposite is still waiting, you can go. But don't be too hasty. It often happens that, as you move, he does too! Don't panic. Either of you can stop easily. If this happens and **B** is turning right, you both go round the imaginary "flag-pole" and each other. Wait at **D** if you need to, while he gets out sufficiently for you then to go behind him. If he is going straight across you still go round the centre point *after he clears*. (He has priority as he is going forwards on his own side of the road – the minor road as here extending across the major one.) If he goes to his left you can tail in behind.

That is the theory.

You stick to it but beware if **B** starts to cut across in front of you. Be ready to stop at **C** if he does. You can go on, round your "flag-pole", after he has gone.

You may however, decide instead, then to "cross in front" too, depending on all the circumstances. I will come to that as promised but not until a few more paragraphs' time. *Normally*, unless there is restricted room and everybody always crosses in front at that particular junction, waiting till you can go on round your "flag-pole" is what you must do.

135

If there is more than one driver waiting to come out from opposite, the 2nd and subsequent ones should wait for you (as discussed on page 124). But they may not! So be prepared to wait at **D**. Afterwards you can go behind them smartly on, following the solid arrow as in fig. 59.

As ever, directly you are under way, move ahead swiftly if you can; check your mirrors straightaway and that your signal has now cancelled itself.

Wherever possible, avoid such waiting at **C** or **D** as has been described, for real danger exists from fast traffic appearing from **H** or **I**.

The danger is from these fast major-road drivers not realising that both you and those opposite you may become temporarily **STUCK** in the middle. Like the lorry driver in fig. 53, they kid themselves before they arrive that their way will be clear, and delay braking until the last second, perhaps too late! Such fools often blare their horns in anger, apparently believing that they have some absolute right to a clear road – a "right" which the law cannot possibly give them. (They should know too, that the only correct use of the horn is to warn someone of your presence.)

If you do get delayed at **C** or **D**, then provided you are established there *long before* any major-road traffic is even in sight, you shouldn't be at any risk. You have arguably as much "right" to sit there as they have to come along.

However, if you shoot out in the teeth of major-road traffic coming, in the vain hope that those opposite will stay still, and *are* then delayed at **C** or **D**, you will have mainly yourself to blame if all the others are not good enough drivers to protect you from your folly.

People behind you, for instance, are likely to move up, blocking off any chance of your retreating.

Were you to be one of those people behind I sincerely hope you would have had the forethought not to do any such thing. Would you?

Leaving The Major Road

Double-check your mirrors, signal, position and slow, as for any **Right Turn** *Off* **A Major Road**. Wait for a gap in the oncoming traffic, and then make your turn going round the imaginary centre point flag-pole of the crossroads (in an exactly similar way to that described above when you are *emerging from the minor road*). Sneak that usual glance over your right shoulder (page 131) that can save you from trouble on two wheels, last thing before you turn.

Right-turning oncoming traffic should play it by the, by now, familiar, *basic rule*, and pass round offside-to-offside behind you. If they don't, for any of the reasons which will become clear in the next section – *Crossing In Front When Turning Right* – then you will have to plan your turn accordingly as stated there.

Any crossing or turning traffic from the minor roads should wait for major-road right-turners to clear before it moves. Should one try to nip out or across be prepared to stop and prevent an accident. Apply forgiveness.

Make your turn swiftly as soon as you are free to do so. Remember not to turn your steering wheels till ready to go on round. Once you are into the turning accelerate smartly unless there are reasons not to; check your mirrors as usual; cancel your indicator if necessary.

A further complication ensues when there is more than one oncoming driver preparing to turn right, and perhaps you are part of a growing right-turning queue too. Alas for a Learner like **U**, in fig. 60, traffic has built up before a gap materialises. If a rotter hoots as you wait keep calm. *A hoot only hurts if you let it.*

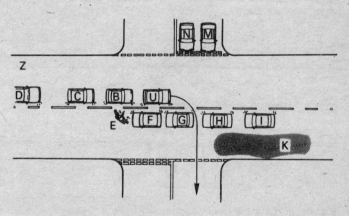

Fig. 60   A problem turning right.

The position in fig. 60 is probably not dangerous as **U** are shielded by the other stopped traffic. The difficulty usually resolves simply, something like this: **E, F** and **G** close up bumper-to-bumper and **H** and **I** wait a little back, leaving a gap for **U**, **B**, **C** and **D** to use. Thus the congestion clears and **E**, **F** and **G**, can make their right turns once traffic from **Z** has ceased, followed by **H** and **I**. Then **M** and **N** are clear to cross if no more traffic arrives along the major road.

U, before taking the gap left to you by **H** and **I**, dare not go without checking area **K**, as must each of those who follow **U**. **U** must edge forward till you can see round **H**. Shoot through, and you can be in a smash before **U** know it.

Crossing In Front When Turning Right

I have thrice referred to this exception to the *basic rule* at crossroads. There are plenty of times when, instead of going round behind the flag-pole when you join a major road (i.e. offside-to-offside viz-a-viz traffic opposite you – as in the *basic rule*), drivers use the alternative of crossing in front, nearside-to-nearside as in fig. 61. The exception originally evolved for crossroads where the weight of traffic or restricted room made sticking to the *basic rule* impractical. Nowadays you will find it happening more and more, and the road markings at some junctions even lay down that you must use the exception. (Such markings are more commonly found at traffic lights but always look out for them.)

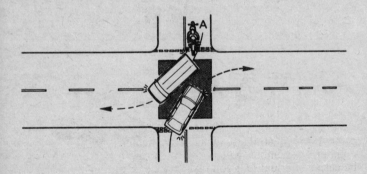

Fig. 61 *Crossing in front* when turning right.

When crossing in front, both turning vehicles must go carefully as they pass each other in the shaded area shown in fig. 61, lest traffic which may be hidden behind their opposite

138

number – *like motorcycle* **A** *to which the car must give way* – springs forward.

It is *because* of this restricted vision, of course, that the *basic rule* has to remain your normal method.

Nevertheless, at every right turn you make at such crossroads, you need to assess how any driver opposite you is going to handle it, and determine your path and actions in the light of what you see beginning to happen. As a Learner don't be first to opt for the exception (unless road markings force you) but be ready to fall in with it straightaway *if appropriate*, if a driver from the other side makes it obvious that that is the way he wants to adopt.

As explained earlier, you should never normally cross in front unless road markings demand it or there is so little room that it is an obvious necessity; so it may *not be appropriate*, despite what an oncoming driver has started to do. In that case you should wait (or move only as far as **C**, fig. 59, providing you were clear left and right), before going on round the flag-pole once you were free to do so, as in the normal *basic rule*.

However, you have to balance the regimented discipline of doing that, with the overall situation and the extra hold-up you may cause people behind you. Sometimes where the driver(s) opposite is/are determined to cross in front anyway, you will be quicker and thus less exposed to fast major-road traffic, if you simply follow suit. Your teacher must be wide-awake to confirm your decisions at first.

Crossing in front may be necessary too, as you *leave* a major road at a crossroads. Here again it's a matter of watching road markings, summing up whatever an oncoming right-turner may do, as well as the overall situation, and then acting as befits the particular circumstances. Because oncoming major-road traffic is likely to be faster, you must be even more careful about "hidden" traffic which is expecting to come through straight ahead from behind your opposite number. Remember, *you must give way to them*. All this may be easier to visualise if you imagine two of the right turners, in fig. 60. trying to pass in front of each other when someone from **K** or **Z** was belting through dangerously fast.

GOING STRAIGHT AHEAD

Assume for the moment that *you are driving along a major road*. As we saw with fig. 53 you are *not* free to ignore all side

139

roads. At all turnings, either side, and particularly at crossroads, be alert. People *often* pull out carelessly. They may just forget to look, or they may look and not see; perhaps a foot slips off a clutch; or maybe they drink and drive. The reasons are endless.

Always slow down in readiness for the remotest chance of trouble. Picking up speed again is easy. The hard thing is stopping when things go wrong.

How much you need to cut your speed – FOR EACH AND EVERY TURN – depends on your present speed, *your* road width, whether there is oncoming traffic, how much you can see into the side road, on your road surface and the weather, and on the space available for avoiding action, and so on. A toot should warn a driver, rider, or someone on foot of your presence if you think that you might not have been seen.

MAKE ALLOWANCES! A junction in town swarming with pedestrians is different from one with none. Crossroads with vision limited by woods, hedges, long grass etc. have to be passed more slowly than ones in open flat countryside. Where a blind turning joins, walking pace – even when you are on the major of the two roads – may be more than enough. OK there will be turnings you may pass without needing to slow down – but never pass by without giving the matter any thought . . .

Whenever someone does pull out across your path – even with plenty of time – ASSUME THAT HE WON'T MAKE IT FULLY OUT OF YOUR WAY *until you can see that he* HAS *done.* Slow sufficiently to stop if ultimately you have to. Not to is madness. You don't want to become a joint victim of anything going wrong for him.

Equally, if someone crossing or turning way ahead is blocking your path because he is having to wait, NEVER ASSUME HE WILL BE ABLE TO MOVE CLEAR BEFORE YOU GET THERE.

As I said before, it's stopping that can so easily elude you. Forging ahead *after* someone *is* clear is simplicity itself. It is your duty to be in control of your speed, to allow for misjudgments.

Remember that a vehicle sallying forth from a turn to your *right*, may cause an oncoming driver suddenly to swing across onto your side . . . What then? Fault hardly stops with the exiting or the oncoming drivers if *you* are coming too fast to take avoiding action.

Another cause for caution is when an oncoming driver may be intending to turn right, into a turn ahead of you on your left. Suppose you are going along a major road minding your own business when such a driver – let's say of a lorry – risks turning right just ahead of and across you. You brake enough to miss him, but then a smaller vehicle behind the lorry commits himself to swing across you as well . . .

In driving, minding your own business is rarely enough. You should have noticed the lorry hadn't been slowing up sufficiently to stop and wait before making his turn. You should have been covering your brake ready; and assuming the unseen risk behind him might be there too – until you saw it was not.

In stop-start traffic, you may notice a driver waiting desperately in a side-road to join yours. Where reasonable, be courteous; slow or stop, and let him out. Help by giving an arm slowing down signal. See page 145. This alerts everyone else too. But don't wave him out. It is for him to decide if it is safe. Stop a little more short than necessary. This helps the driver coming out to see that no one is trying to pass you (and hopefully anyone so silly as to attempt that, to see why you have stopped!).

I now consider what to do when *you want to go straight ahead at a crossroads where you are on the minor road*. As with **Right Turns At Crossroads** (where you are emerging from the minor road), even when the sign only commands that you GIVE WAY, it is better for a Learner to stop in any event.

Give yourself the extra time to look all ways properly.

Slow down, getting down as far as 3rd gear, just as you would for any junction where you intend to stop. Remember all I have said about eyeball work on approach to the line, at the line, *and* as you go across. The examiner will want to see you taking account of what anyone opposite is doing. He is watching to see that no one from either direction along the major road will be caused to slow because of your crossing.

You will see over-confident drivers spurt across major roads when traffic coming along them is much too near. Never copy. They make no allowance for the unforeseen, for example, sudden drive-shaft failure.

Instead, make it your own additional iron-rule **NEVER TO DRIVE ACROSS ANYONE'S SAFE STOPPING DISTANCE.** It's a life-saver.

Which Queue?

Where two lanes in which to form queues are marked at the end of a minor road (or where there is room for two even though they are not marked), if you are going straight across you can choose either one – unless an arrow on the road reserves it for turning traffic. Subject to no problem in your mirrors choose an appropriate lane early, position accordingly and stick to that. In the absence of other factors the righthand lane is normally best; using it, quite often allows left-turning traffic to filter away, whilst you (or anyone turning right), would have to wait. Never straddle two lanes. That's selfish.

No indicator signals are appropriate when going straight on. However, see *Arriving At A Major Road* under **Arm Signals Timing,** shortly; an arm signal may occasionally be useful.

LANE DECISIONS FOR JUNCTIONS

Up to this stage of discussing your handling of junctions I have made but brief mention of *pre*-selecting an appropriate lane; I have simply referred to queueing in the appropriate part of the road as necessary, for example when turning right, or wherever else there is room for separate queues.

Many major roads, particularly in towns, often have two or more lanes each way. As was explained in **PART TWO**, there may be KEEP LEFT bollards every so often, but there is no central reservation separating each direction, so these are not dual carriageways. (DUAL CARRIAGEWAY JUNCTIONS will be discussed later.)

On these multi-lane major roads you must pre-select the appropriate lane, if you are not in it already, long before you want to make a turn off. Because **Lane Discipline** rules as in **PART TWO** apply to such lane changes, you have to operate a long, long way ahead. The object is to be in lane well in advance of the point that you will start to signal for your turn itself. Otherwise you may be unable to take your planned route!

If you are going straight ahead, then all the considerations given just now, at the start of GOING STRAIGHT AHEAD, apply, with added care if you are "hemmed-in" to your lane by traffic alongside as you pass through the junction. Make sure you are not in the process of overtaking as you pass through it . . . see page 163.

A minor road with two lanes each way, though less common, may equally require a prior lane change well before you arrive at a junction with a main road, depending on your intended direction. The two lanes each way may only be the case near to the junction itself, and they may be unmarked; good drivers simply create them if there is room.

HERRING-BONE TRAFFIC-SEPARATION LINES

Fig. 62 shows a simple example of how these are often used to create a safe "sanctum" for turning traffic off a major road. On wider major roads such as those just described, as well as on plenty of quite wide roads but which have only one wide lane each way, through traffic is channelled to the outsides of a herring-boned area at more dangerous junctions. Well before the white-painted "sanctum", large arrows in the centre of the major road forewarn every driver who is *not* turning, to move aside and make a single file as they pass the junction. This allows anyone who *is* turning, to move into the sanctum and wait there safely if they have to; they are sheltered there from fast through traffic, all of which can scarcely be unaware that there is a junction, and that they must not be overtaking. Traffic exiting from the turning is also able to shelter.

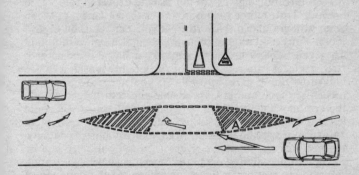

Fig. 62 Herring bone traffic-separation lines protecting turners.

There are many variations in the ways that these "sanctums" are set out in respect of priorities for the turning traffic

143

which is using them. The position of GIVE WAY lines may, for example, indicate at a crossroads layout, that *Crossing In Front* is expected. You need to study some live examples in your area and relate them to the *basic rules* I have given you. Compare these "sanctums" with the *SAFE AREA* for turners of dual carriageway turns too. The fundamental principles for using *them*, come a little later in this **PART THREE**.

The outside edge of these "sanctums" is painted with a broken line. Continuous lines around these herring-bone stripes would make a widened double white line. *You do find the latter at brows of hills etc. and it is illegal to drive onto them*. Technically, however, you can drive over the striped part of a "sanctum". I would *only* normally do so if I was turning right off the major road. Then I might move over into the "sanctum" a little early, using area **A** of the stripes in fig. 62. Doing so can be a help to through traffic. It can save them having to slow down unnecessarily much, behind you, before you move over. However I suggest you leave such advanced courtesy till after your Test.

ARM SIGNALS

Arm direction signals are not usually expected to be used on your Test, either for turns, for changing lanes, or when going straight ahead. Nevertheless you can be asked to give them. You could require them if your indicators were to fail. They can be very useful to reinforce a flashing indicator if circumstances are unusual, or in bright sunshine when indicators don't show up well. So you need to be able to recognise them, and at least be able yourself to demonstrate the arm movements which they entail. Otherwise you could be at a loss if you have to use one on the move, or if, in answer to a specific question from your examiner, you need to show how one should be given.

Therefore I will first detail the "mechanics" of each signal, returning to matters of timing after that. At the same time I will include the all-important *slowing down* arm signal which, as already noted, you *are expected* to use at any appropriate time during your Test.

You should appreciate that an arm signal *alone*, is not always seen. You can reckon that anyone the wrong side of your car won't see you give it.

So always add the appropriate indicator. Never think of an arm signal as a substitute (except one to be used with immense care should your indicators break down).

If giving a straight-on, or a left, arm signal **from inside the car**, (see below), never rely on *everyone* seeing that, either.

Arm Right Turn Signal

Get three-quarters of your arm *straight* out at right angles to your car with closed fingers extended. Face your palm towards the oncoming traffic. Hold the arm steady.

Arm Left Turn Signal

This signal needs exaggerated arm movement. Use a continuous forwards circular motion (i.e. anti-clockwise) with your elbow bending – rather like a crawl swimmer and at much the same speed.

Arm Slowing Down Signal

Give a whole metre of up-and-down movement *from the shoulder*, with your arm and hand out straight and your palm downwards. A smooth down-and-up beat to match your own steady heartbeat is ideal.

Arm Signals **From Inside Car** Mainly To Police, Etc.

See your Highway Code illustrations for these signals. Your hand should be as close to the windscreen as is practical to help the signal be seen at once.

ARM SIGNALS TIMING

Perhaps the most vital aspect of timing, when you are putting your arm out of your window, is to make sure you never do so at a moment when it could be wiped off!

For the timing of an arm *slowing down signal* please refer back to page 84.

For arm *turn* signals, first refresh your memory of *positioning*, speed and gear procedure at junctions, all from the beginning of this **PART THREE**. As these factors are always similar, an arm signal timing "system" can flow from them.

Arriving At A Major Road

If you intend to cross over and go *straight ahead*, no direction arm signal is normally appropriate on the approach. Nor is one necessary if, when you arrive, all is clear and you have no need to stop.

145

If you do have to stop when you get there, then there may subsequently be a need for an arm straight-ahead signal **from inside the car** while you are waiting, either for the benefit of someone controlling traffic or of someone waiting opposite, or, possibly, to inform someone **behind** you of your intention. You have to judge how useful it might be, and your teacher can help. The main use of the signal is to help officers on point-duty, and it need only be given briefly till you see they have understood. Work on the basis someone may not have noted your signal unless you have seen a nod or acknowledgement.

When you are *turning* into a major road, an arm direction signal, if you are giving them in addition to indicators, is then always appropriate. It needs to be given quite well in advance of the event. You cannot flap your arm in-and-out of the window and change gear at the same time because **AT LEAST ONE HAND MUST BE ON THE WHEEL** *at all times*. You don't want to be giving it during the last few metres when you should be concentrating on eyeball work. Therefore the "system" it is best to follow, for left or right turns, is always to give your signal as soon as you are down into 3rd gear, before any further gear change may be needed. One signal, given long enough to be noticed, is normally enough.

For a right turn it is best to change down a bit early, so that you can begin to signal before starting to move out towards the centre line at the end of the road.

The only time you might repeat your arm signal would be if you had had a long wait (as might be the case at traffic lights, for example) before you could get out into the major road; in that event repeat it briefly just before your **Smooth Start**, so that any new arrivals will know where you are going.

If that is a right repeat signal – do take care of that arm . . . If it is for a left turn, this repeat signal might be more conveniently and appropriately given in the style noted above for giving **from inside the car.**

Leaving A Major Road

Arm direction signalling for turning off a major road can follow an exactly similar "system" – giving the signal once, directly you are down to 3rd gear, long enough for all to see (and only as an adjunct to normal indicators unless they have gone wrong). Again, for right turns, change down a bit early to allow time to commence the signal before you begin to move out to your crown-of-the-road position. Again, unless you are having to wait for a long time in the middle before you can complete your right turn, to give any repeat arm signal is here probably unnecessary. As before, keeping your arm intact may have to take precedence over the signalling if traffic is flashing by close to you!

MORE TRICKY JUNCTIONS

WHEN A LATE SIGNAL IS CORRECT

In fig. 63, to avoid confusion with the crossing shortly before **YOUR TURNING**, only begin your signal from area **A**. Nor should **U** begin to move closer to the kerb till you reach **A**. However, slow down normally. Then no one arriving at or waiting to join the major road, or to turn right off it at the crossroads, should ever mistake where you want to go, and perhaps pull out or across, in front of you in error.

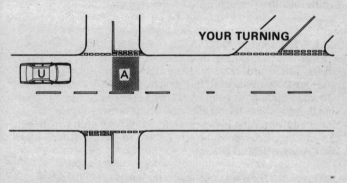

Fig. 63   When a late signal is correct.

In fig. 64 you are **U**. If going left at **Z** you should have been summing up the situation and lining up what will become unmistakable positioning for your turn, from long before **A**. As just pointed out, you will be wise only to start a left signal *as you pass* **B**. Nevertheless your careful positioning line, following the broken arrow, and slowing down appropriately for entry to **Z** rather than **Y**, should ensure drivers **B, C** and **D** recognize your intentions correctly. Lorry **D**, correctly positioned ready to go to **Y**, waits as shown until he is sure what **U** are doing! He is particularly careful not to edge forward prematurely on what would turn out to be a false premise – i.e. that **U** would be going into **Y**.

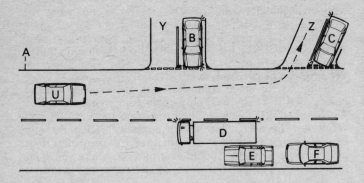

Fig. 64   Skilled positioning to back up signals.

MAKE NO ASSUMPTIONS

B, in fig. 64, waiting to come out left watches your front wheels, disregarding your left indicator if it's on. Suppose **U** have left your indicator flashing by mistake? Or you have naughtily changed your mind without remembering your signal was on? Only if he saw those wheels turn and **U** physically entering his own road would he prepare to go. (Even then he would be ever-wary to watch for anyone hidden close behind **U** . . .)

Never trust the indicator; watch the wheels.

B would probably start as soon as **U** have passed, but must look out that he doesn't then collide with **C**. **C** should have earlier noted **B's** preparation to join the major road and been ready to wait for him. But suppose **C** had arrived in a hurry, too late for that anyway, or for **B** to know he was there? Excited by an apparent chance to tail in neatly behind **F**, **C** might simply have decided to risk moving out during the split-second or so while **B** was masked by **U**. Bang! Bad boys both, **C** and **B** . . . each for assuming there was nothing hidden beyond **U** **at the crucial moment.**

148

TURNING LEFT AND, ALMOST IMMEDIATELY, RIGHT

In fig. 65 **U** are in road **A**, preparing to get to road **B**. Imagine that **D** – **E** is chock-a-block both ways with dense, *slow* traffic – more than I can show here. Notice that there are two lanes on each side of it. Wait till both the lanes to your right are clear, and then move smartly. Following the arrowed path, take up an immediate right turn "line", changing your indicator signal direction from left to right straightaway at **G** so that everyone can spot your intention at once. Be prepared to have to wait at **C** for a gap in approaching traffic before you can complete your turn.

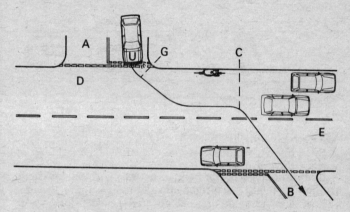

Fig. 65   Staggered crossing.

If initially the nearest lane to **U** coming from **D**, clears, but the outer one is still full of stop-start traffic moving up all the time, it may be safe – guided by your teacher – to edge out to **G**, change your indicator and then wait there. Wait till the second lane clears too, or someone in it stops to let you go, before you carry on to **C** etc.

Fresh traffic arriving in the nearer lane from **D** should pull up calmly if you are still waiting at **G**; however, see also page 136.

TURNING RIGHT AND, ALMOST IMMEDIATELY, LEFT

Normally, you must wait for the road to clear *both ways* before you can complete this "double" turn in one operation.

Your "line" this time will be along the arrowed path of fig.
66. You change your indicator to the left directly after
leaving your minor road.

In "rush-hour" conditions, however, traffic sometimes
never seems to clear both ways at once! U may need to move
out into position A, in fig. 66, during a clear moment from
the right and then wait there, by now indicating left.

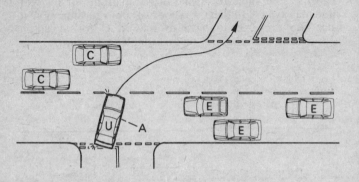

Fig. 66   A little courtesy goes a long way.

Before doing that you have to ensure that none amongst
traffic C wants to turn right into the road you are leaving.
(Those leaving a major road generally have priority over
those joining, so you can't just move out into an immediate
clash with them.)

New traffic E, if any, then has to wait. Hopefully it will
thoughtfully do so a good bit short of the junction so that
U can see well past the front stopped vehicle(s) in case some
idiot attempts to pass it/them. U are now ready to go ahead
immediately the last of traffic C goes by.

Sometimes (rather than all C traffic clearing at once) a C
driver will then come along who does want to turn right; and
he will kindly stop a little short of his normal right turn
position, so that you can get away first, shielded to some
extent from further traffic behind him. That you can do;
however, it will be your lookout to see that it is safe and that
there is no inside lane C traffic still to worry about. Such C
traffic may or may not, stop politely too.

All this depends on considerate driving all round. To begin

with your teacher must advise you on every step. You must temper the Highway Code advice not to block any junction, with commonsense in all the circumstances. If you are going to move out and wait with your car across a major-road lane, do so only when traffic in it has stopped for you, or when there is no one in sight coming. It is *exceedingly dangerous* to try to edge out more and more, in the hope that someone may stop.

Later on you will be able to give an appropriate grateful nod to those who help you, which a Learner is not expected to give, but remember then, *never to sacrifice concentration and attention* on **LOOKING WHERE YOU ARE GOING.**

HEADLAMP FLASHING

When they want to be polite by waiting as just described (or in other situations), some drivers also flash their headlamps so as to indicate that you can go. The trouble is some rude drivers may flash aggressively, meaning that *they* are going to go! Also, flashes are frequently taken by the *wrong persons* (not necessarily even drivers) as being *meant for them.* My advice is to be guided by what drivers and other road users DO, not by someone's light-flashes. Look at what your Highway Code says on this subject too.

Some drivers flash their headlamps to inform drivers going the other way that there is a police speed trap. The practice is illegal.

DUAL CARRIAGEWAY JUNCTIONS

THE *SAFE AREA* FOR TURNERS

The opening through the central reservation, shaded in fig. 67, is the *SAFE AREA*. It is with your car fully encapsulated on here that, if need be, you wait, sheltered from fast traffic *both ways.*

Increasingly, such gaps on duals for turning or crossing, are either being closed, or re-designed to allow fewer options. Many were *black spots* (fatal accident sites) anyway. Nevertheless, to save space and unneeded extra explanations, my examples which follow are based on two fully open junctions, so that you can absorb the *basic rules* for every kind of layout you may meet. These will be the rules to fall back on wherever road markings are not demanding different posi-

tioning or procedure, or where the actions of others make it
sensible to adapt the way you operate.

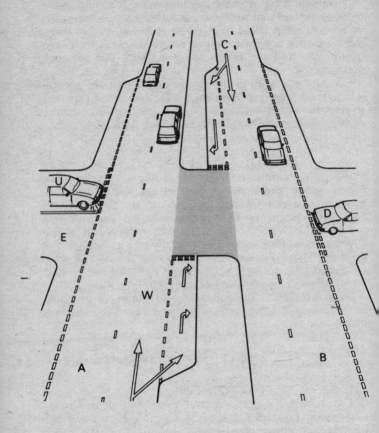

Fig. 67   Dual carriageway *SAFE AREA* for turners.

TURNS *ONTO* A DUAL CARRIAGEWAY

Leftward joining should be simple. Just be sure to gauge
how very quickly, traffic from your right may be coming.
Make sure that there will be no chance of your engine stalling
and be geared to accelerate purposefully into the lefthand
lane up to a suitable speed. People can appear in your

152

mirrors at lightning speed on duals, so you can rapidly be in danger unless you pick up speed quickly.

However, in your concentration to your right, never forget pedestrians who may stride off the pavement to your left.

If there is a length of acceleration slip road to help you get onto the dual, use it. Be it short or quite long, it is often possible to "time it" so that you begin accelerating on the slip road, and can then tail in neatly into a gap as you merge out onto the dual. Gaps shorter than could otherwise be used from a standing start can then be used; however, your teacher must guide at first.

To time your acceleration on such a slip road accurately, it is essential to *look over your right shoulder* as well as in your mirrors. But watch out for anyone in front of you and also trying to merge, suddenly coming to an unexpected stop! Believe me they often do . . .

Depending upon the length and the angle of the slip road, and the speed of traffic on the dual, you need to be in 2nd or 3rd gear as you merge on to it. Aim to be neatly within the peak pulling power range (see fig. 4) of the appropriate gear so that you won't need to change up again till you are safely onto the dual carriageway.

The "name of the game" with these merges is to have reached the same speed as the traffic on the dual before or as you merge in. Then it should be easy, safe and simple.

As a rule when you are turning left onto a dual carriage-way, if someone opposite you is waiting in the *SAFE AREA* to complete a right turn, let them go first. Remember that they will be coming across into the left lane of the dual. See also page 124.

When you turn right *onto* a dual the *basic rule* of passing drivers from opposite, offside-to-offside, applies, unless road markings dictate otherwise. Here that passing occurs, of course, on the *SAFE AREA*. Be very careful about any *crossing in front;* see below.

If the *SAFE AREA* for you in the middle is still full – **OR POTENTIALLY FULL** – don't budge from your minor road yet. Wait till there will be room for your entire car length to stop on there in safety. Note that, so far as **U** are concerned in fig. 67, anyone coming from the left, i.e. from **C**, takes priority. They are leaving the major road. They are *potential fillers* of the *SAFE AREA*, to be looked out for *before* you consider leaving your minor road.

Sometimes, where a deceleration slip road has been

created for them to run off the dual itself – so as to afford them greater safety prior to their actual turn – GIVE WAY lines, as in my fig. 67, theoretically then hold them at the edge of the *SAFE AREA*, while you come out onto it. But my view is never count on that! If they move forward at just the wrong moment you'll be in a far more deadly pickle (having to leave your boot sticking out) than they will. So, whilst studying the road markings and following whatever they lay down, study more carefully, what others DO!

Suppose U are turning right into dual road **B** in fig. 67, and dual **A** clears first. Assuming you're OK to get onto the *SAFE AREA* (see above), you can now nip over and wait on the left side of it. You may then have to wait *after dual* **B** *clears* while **D** crosses to beside you. Technically, as ever, he expects you to go round behind him on your way to complete your turn *correctly into the left lane of* **B**. As with leftward joining above, take care that your subsequent **Smooth Start**, off the *SAFE AREA* is equally well disciplined against a stall, and that you accelerate with some gusto once you are into **B**, checking your mirrors immediately, clicking off your indicator if you need to.

As with any right turn be prepared for some nut on two wheels (or in this case on 4, or more!) to come up on your righthand side from behind, just as you are about to complete your turn. Because of the extra room the *SAFE AREA* often allows, I'm afraid it becomes *more* likely. Don't get mixed up with them. Let them go. A neat flash-look out of the corner of your right eye at the right moment should spot them coming. They may be attempting a shifty *Crossing In Front* manoeuvre; see below.

Note that there is no need to stop on the *SAFE AREA* at all if the entire area and dual **B** is already clear. Just get on.

Crossing In Front on the *SAFE AREA* as you turn right onto a dual carriageway is another possibility to contend with, if there are people opposite you, themselves wanting to turn right. See page 138. Tackle it as explained there, laced with self-preservation! If there is the slightest doubt about what someone opposite will do when they get onto the *SAFE AREA*, do not head over there yourself yet. The chance of being caught half-way on, exposed at your rear to high speed traffic, is too serious to take.

I said four paragraphs above that you complete your turn "*correctly into the left lane of* **B**". Sometimes, during heavy traffic, you will see drivers head into the righthand lane instead. They are usually ones who have also *crossed in front* on the *SAFE AREA*. Instead of waiting for both lanes from **C**, fig. 67, to become clear, they just wait for the outside one to be empty and scoot into it, accelerating like a scalded cat. Although the growing popularity of this manoeuvre undoubtedly serves to speed up traffic flow at busy times, the legality of the move could be difficult to prove. Leave it to others unless you are prepared to argue in Court!

Note that if arriving in the outside lane from **C** yourself, you must be prepared to have it happen in front of you, wrong as it may be.

Extraordinary mistakes can happen at night and in fog. Suppose in fig. 67 **U** turn to **W**, not realising it is a dual carriageway. You can imagine the result! Signs and layout should prevent errors. But especially at such times be on your guard.

TURNS *OFF* A DUAL CARRIAGEWAY

Lane Discipline is vital here because higher traffic speeds make any sudden moves very risky. If you are going to have to move lanes for your turn (back into the left one or over to a right one) this must be *complete well before* the point where you are anticipating slowing down for the turn itself. It would be rude and dangerous to slow up immediately after overtaking someone, and thoroughly dangerous to do so no sooner than having joined a fast-trafficked righthand lane. If you cannot achieve such a lane change adequately in time as a separate prior operation, it is usually best to abandon the turn. The safety of fast traffic behind – and your own – is at stake.

Leftward leaving should need no further explanation except to reiterate that deceleration slip roads are there to be used! Move fully into a slipway from the *first possible moment*. Plenty are built extra long so that much of your slowing down can be done on there anyway. Avoid hampering everyone else.

Fig. 68 shows a right turn *off* a dual. Wait in the forward half of the *SAFE ARFA away* from you, as shown, leaving room for anyone such as **A**, wanting to turn right, to come out onto it, beside you. If the *SAFE AREA* is in use wait near the front of the deceleration slip road, close in, like car **B**, till it clears for you. If you cannot yet finish your turn anyway, be prepared to let others through, as in fig. 60.

If a deceleration slip road off to the right – designed for

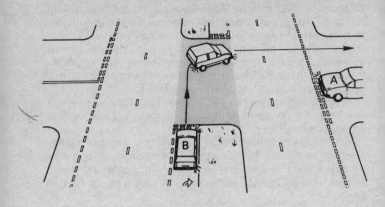

Fig. 68 Right turns off dual carriageways.

your safety – is *itself* full, or in danger of so being, you *must* anticipate this, several hundred metres further ahead even than usual. Then your extra early signal *and* slowing down can forewarn those behind you that you may be having to stop in the fast lane . . .

Unfortunately, correct positioning in the *SAFE AREA* as above, can (as ever) encourage idiots from behind to move up on your righthand side. They hope to nip ahead off the *SAFE AREA* before you move. Right or wrong, let them.

DO UNTO OTHERS . . .

As you drive along a dual carriageway you can often help anyone joining it from the left to come in earlier. If it is clear behind you simply move out one lane well in advance of the junction. You move back later. The goodwill gesture enhances your own safety too, against the chance he might have moved forward accidentally. The *planned avoidance of danger* here combines with doing unto other drivers as you would have them do unto you.

As you pass through dual carriageway junctions, going straight on, YOU must be prepared for any of the mistakes or pitfalls I have described, to happen to people who are crossing or turning.

Truly in these circumstances, speed kills. Control yours.

TRAFFIC LIGHTS

Study the traffic-light rules in the Highway Code. Go to busy lights, stand and watch. Notice the *sequence* of the lights even if you *think* you know. Review the lights from the point of view of pedestrians too. Think about what those on foot ought to do. Observe what sort of things they DO do.

You probably won't have to stay long in order to see some drivers "shoot" the lights, that is, cross when they ought to have/be stopped. Either they will be rushing ahead before green appears or they will be attempting to keep going and squeeze through after amber has come up. The 2-wheeled fraternity, you will note, weave in-and-out of slow traffic, turn "against" red, etc., with apparent impunity. All these are "streetwise" matters which concern you . . . At the wheel your eyes cannot afford to miss a trick ahead, either side, or in your mirrors.

APPROACHING TRAFFIC LIGHTS

Mirrors, signalling, positioning, and slowing and selecting the right gear, can all be handled at traffic lights in a similar way to the methods used at crossroads, with a few adjustments as below.

Approaching Lights When Intending To Go Straight On

Imagine in fig. 69 U are doing a shade under 30 m.p.h. and *will be going straight on*. Long before you reach the lights your long-range searching eye (and your prior study/experience) will have told you what colour they are likely to be when you reach them.

For instance, if the lights *change to green* when U are only 200 metres away and with no one between you and the lights, as at fig. 69, F, you can expect they will stay green till you have passed through them.

Mind you, a few lights change again remarkably quickly, so be warned!

However, normally, if green appears at this stage with little traffic and a clear road – as would be the case in fig. 69 were you to delete all the shaded cars for the time being – there will be no need to drop below 25 m.p.h. You judge how fast is safe allowing for the road width and for your stopping ability in such an event as that a pedestrian like one of those at Z, or maybe the one at Q, might step into your path. Take 3rd gear at G to give you acceleration "in hand". That will ensure that, even if you do have to slow down a bit more –

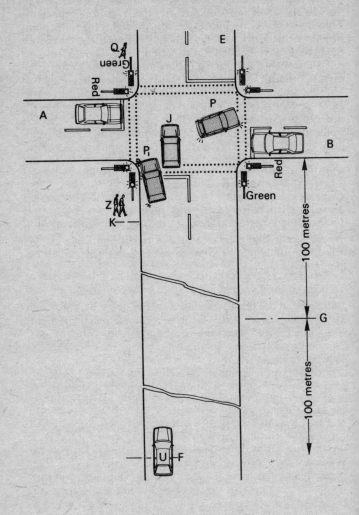

Fig. 69 Traffic light timing.

say until you are certain **Q** won't step out – you can pick up the speed straightaway as you pass the last danger point. Neither the pedestrians at **Z** nor the one at **Q** should try to cross in front of **U**; after all red will be shining in their direction. But do remember that there are plenty of exceptional pedestrians!

Alternatively, if you expect the light to be amber and then red before you reach it, you prepare to stop. Take 3rd gently from **F**, then down to 2nd gear by **G**, 100 metres before the lights. You are ready to stop but, by being in 2nd, you are also furnished with the pulling power should the light unexpectedly remain green, to carry on through, keeping up your speed appropriately.

It is correct to continue on amber *only if there is no time to stop safely*. But never go through on red. If amber appears when you are around **K**, in fig. 69, take the lesser risk – going or stopping – judging by traffic conditions. You should already be in the correct gear, if to go on is safer. It is undisciplined driving to land yourself in an emergency stop for red. The streetwise anticipation here above is the best way to prevent it. To approach a green traffic light above 35–40 m.p.h., even if it was one the phasing of which you knew well and it was in a wide open space with no other people or vehicles around, would be too fast. The situation can alter too quickly. Hence, although there are lights at which a little faster is safe, my descriptions range around an approach of 30 m.p.h. or slower.

Approaching Lights When Intending To Turn

Return to fig. 69 and imagine this time that **U** are *going to turn at the lights*. Right or left there can now be pedestrians to whom you must expect to GIVE WAY. They are indeed likely to step out to walk across the road **A–B** just as you want to enter it. Traffic along **A–B** has stopped *for them*, as well as for the **E–F** traffic. For their direction of walking the lights are showing *green*. Whereas, instantly **U** begin to turn into **A–B** you are then moving "against" the red light of **A–B**, albeit properly and legally to make your turn. Therefore you must be prepared to stop for them at **P** or **P₁**, only completing your turn once the way is clear or they are obviously going to wait while you go. If there is *anyone* in the vicinity on foot, your speed must be down to a mere trickle at the point of turning. You are thus ready (as always) to allow them the "red carpet treatment" reserved for kings, should they wish to cross.

Suppose **U** are going to turn right in fig. 69. You may well first have to wait at **J** before going round "through traffic" from **E**. (Or wait a little less far forward if *Crossing In Front* is going to be appropriate.) Either way, if there are pedestrians walking across road **A–B** – for whom you will have to wait – do not move to **P** until there is *no* traffic coming from **E** however far distant, or until what there is, is already clearly stopping because the lights are now changing again. Otherwise, if a green phase for **E–F** is long, you can easily find yourself blocking the through traffic unnecessarily.

WAITING AT LIGHTS

Because of the relatively long wait usual at red light stops you should nearly always bring your handbrake on once you stop, and then come out of gear. You should certainly do so whenever you are the first to reach the lights. (Should pedestrians then come flocking by closely around in front of or behind your car, as is their wont at traffic light queues, you cannot run into them through any temporary lapse of concentration on your feet.)

However, it is as well to do so anyway. You are then able to follow with relaxing your legs by releasing your foot pedals. This has the added bonuses of removing brakelight eyestrain for people behind (the glare can be considerable in wet weather or in darkness), and of preventing wear within your clutch operating mechanism.

If you are first to arrive pull *gently* right up to the solid white stop line. Avoid leaving several metres of unnecessary gap. That just wastes time for everyone when the lights go green again.

While waiting keep an eye in your mirrors so you are up-to-date there. Also watch the lights facing the crossing traffic if you can see them, as well as for when that traffic itself, if any, starts to pull up. That helps you anticipate amber reappearing for your queue, this time with red still there. For that is the moment to take 1st and prepare for a **Smooth Start**. You are thus ready as soon as green comes on, to go without delay.

However, if you are at the front you must never "jump the gun"! Never assume that green means "go". It doesn't. See your Highway Code. A pedestrian walking across (which can happen anywhere in the queue) is still king! If he is there, don't take 1st till he is clear. And you still have to watch that

160

no wheeled-maniac is shooting through across your bows on amber (or red!).

After *any* moments of waiting, you must, if you are turning – or even shifting position within your own lane – make a final rapid glance over your appropriate shoulder first, to make sure you are not going to knock some rider off his mount. (This *includes* moments held up at **P** or **P₁** as above, in fig. 69.) Always Give Way to them. These two-wheeled pests (the ones who push their luck too far) infest lights.

MORE TO WATCH OUT FOR AT LIGHTS

Clogged traffic is common at traffic lights. As well as obeying the light signals, help others, as explained with fig. 60, whenever you can. This is akin to following *Box Junction* rules which you will find in Question and Answer 14 in **PART FOUR.** Where the yellow criss-cross lines of these are painted at lights, you must stick fully to those rules too. However, as they are commonsense and *should be applied to all junctions anyway* (as urged in your Highway Code), that shouldn't be difficult. We shouldn't need hundreds of litres of yellow paint to tell us not to block junctions – whether they have traffic lights or not. I would love to save the paint to tip over the drivers who do it!

The next snag can happen at other junctions but it seems to be most common at red lights. A large lorry is waiting at the front but there is room to move up on its left. **Beware!** It could be turning left! It simply needs the extra room to do so. Be very sure that won't be the case before you consider squeezing up there to the front.

A Little Right Relief

At many lights turning right is made easier. A phasing adjustment allows several right-turners through after other traffic stops, before renewing priority for the crossing direction. Where that hasn't been built in, courtesy and sense have to suffice.

Arrows On The Road

As in fig. 70 enormous arrows often indicate which lane(s) is/are reserved for your direction. Knowing the road enables you to take the correct lane early but it is easy to be "on the arrows" before seeing what is expected.

Don't panic or swerve if wrong; from what you know of positioning you should be in a reasonable place for your

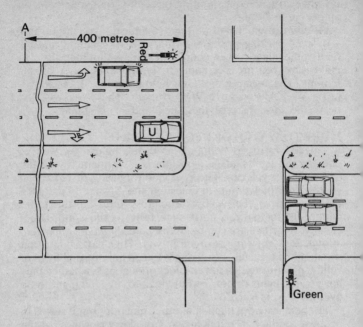

Fig. 70 Arrows on the road.

intended path and drivers around should be careful on seeing your L-plates. Check mirrors, then signal. Double-check your mirrors with a swift glance over your respective shoulder, and then gradually correct your position if you can, remembering your **Lane Discipline.** Unless there is time and a gap to do this you may need to jettison your intended direction, and take a line the arrow on the road says you *can*, adding a signal if necessary. You can always find your way back en route later. You will thus avoid holding up and annoying following traffic. To ignore an arrow can place you the wrong side of the law too.

Look at **U** in fig. 70. Assume you intend to go straight on. If not already in lane by **A**, 400 metres out, then, allowing for traffic behind and perhaps beside you, ease to the middle or right lane immediately you safely can. Always signal the lane change. Cancel that indicator immediately its purpose is over. You are correct in either of these lanes for going straight on, as each has an ahead arrow.

Your choice will depend on what lane you were in to start with, naturally. But it may also depend on whether the middle lane is relatively full and/or on whether anyone ahead may be turning right. However, do remember that in queues you are not allowed to chop and change purely selfishly. See **Lane Discipline** in **PART TWO.**

Once positioned you can concentrate on what colour(s) the lights will be when you arrive, and drive accordingly.

On a multi-lane carriageway it is sometimes difficult to avoid passing through traffic lights almost exactly alongside another vehicle. This can reduce your vision to that side dramatically. Try to time things so that you retain that view by being just ahead, or else drop sufficiently back to be well sheltered from that quarter. Remember that the sight-lines of the person(s) you are alongside must be considered too. The Highway Code rule never to be overtaking at *any* road junction should here be forefront in your mind – applied in a manner consistent with the degree of danger and with the width of carriageway available to all parties.

Banned Routes, Obligatory Routes

A great many traffic lights combine with other signs giving orders: no entry, no left (or right) turn, no U-turn; ahead only, turn left (or right), are common examples. Look out for them. They must be obeyed. They are often, though not always, mounted on the traffic light post itself.

Green Filter Arrows

These allow traffic in one lane to go while red stops others, or a separate filter allows them to flow as well. They can apply to left, right and sometimes to straight ahead traffic.

If a green filter suddenly shows your lane can go, *go* where it points (if safe), *even if you have made a mistake in choosing the lane and don't want to!* You must not hold up correctly positioned followers. Fig 71 shows a simple example.

If Red Reappears Before You Get Clear

At a light you may find that, although you have moved partly forward for a right turn, a chance to complete your turn does not offer until after the lights have again turned amber (from green). Fortunately, there is then usually time before red comes on (see fig. 60, this time imagining there

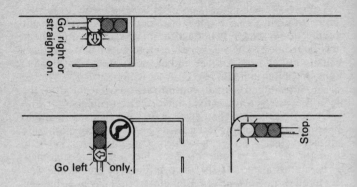

Fig. 71 A green filter arrow.

were lights), for **U, B, E, F** and **G** to take 1st and turn.

C, in fig. 60, not yet up to where the light's stop line would be, waits, as do **H** and **I**. If there is space behind them, **H** and **I** could drop back if necessary, to help everybody trying to clear to get round. **M** and **N** would have little choice but to wait for all this to happen.

In these circumstances it would be bad luck if a speed merchant either shot off on amber (+ red) or was so discourteous as not to give an **L**-driver time. If it happens, stop, wait, and let the experienced drivers circumnavigate you till the position opens. Were you to be hit whilst stationary it ought not to be judged your fault. Then your teacher can guide you as to whether to go on, keep waiting till the lights change again, or back up – whatever is appropriate. *Remember you can wait;* every red light has a green lining!

LEAVING LIGHTS WHEN TURNING
By now, I hope it is no longer necessary to remind you, as you pick up speed as smartly as traffic allows in the new road, to return at once to your **Mirrors, Mirrors, Mirrors** drivestyle drummed in from the beginning of **PART TWO**, and to check that your signal has self-cancelled.

164

POLICEMEN ON POINT DUTY
Traffic Wardens

Learn the meaning of *their* signals and the correct ones to *give them* from your Highway Code. See also **Arm Signals** earlier in this **PART THREE**. They pop up to control traffic where temporary crowds gather, where traffic lights have failed, etc. Do as you are told, stop, or go – *if safe* – remember policemen make mistakes, though rarely. And an accident could be deemed your lookout.

Turning right you would go "round" a constable or warden if he was standing at the centre-point of a crossroads, unless he directed you in front; he would give an obvious sign.

ONE-WAYS

One-way traffic tends to move faster and (to some extent) to crowd the lefthand lane. Perhaps drivers feel more comfortable sticking to their normal side. Nevertheless, you need to learn to use the most appropriate lane which is free for your direction, whichever side that is, or to use a middle lane when that makes sense. When you are in a righthand lane, drivers joining your one-way from a street that side, may not appreciate they are joining a one-way, and may well be looking the WRONG WAY as they arrive to enter. Watch out for those dangerous types who seem automatically to stick their bonnet out a bit too – before looking!

You need to become used to having traffic pass you on the left when you are in a righthand lane, or even on *both* sides at once when you are in a middle lane – especially 2-wheeled traffic. Equally, you must overcome the strangeness of yourself legitimately passing other traffic on its left from time to time. And you must be prepared to make a right turn like U are going to in fig. 72 – from all the way over into the righthand lane – not from the usual crown-of-the-road position. You will see plenty of sleepy drivers fall into that trap!

The key thing if you ever have a doubt what to do next is to *keep to the lane you are in.* Slow down. Stop if necessary. But keep in lane.

Only move from your own lane after having double-checked your mirrors and signalled, and when a flash-look over the relevant shoulder confirms it is safe.

Never wander, or straddle two lanes. You will find most drivers do stay in lane well; and that they hold a steady

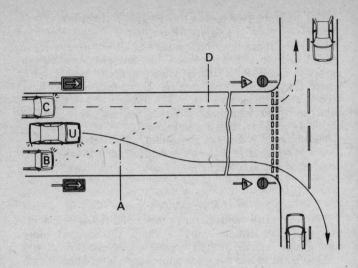

Fig. 72 A one-way scrap?

course even where no lanes are marked.

Should you ever leave a change of lane too late and thus make reaching a turning-off that you wanted, difficult, go on till you can find another one that you can move into lane for, in time. Find your way back to your original choice of road afterwards. Never hold up a busy one-way. They are designed to *ease* congestion and *stimulate* traffic-flow!

MERGING INTO LANE

In fig. 72 **U** want to turn right. Limitations of scale in my picture mean I must ask you to imagine that **U**, **B** and **C** are much less near to the end of the one-way than is apparent at first sight. Count the artist's break in the one-way as a good 75 metres; indeed more would be better unless unusual circumstances made earlier lane changing impracticable.

What happens at **A** and **D**, where the paths of the different parties merge, will depend on the timing and, quite often, on the degree of give-and-take shown by those concerned. As explained under **Lane Discipline** in **PART TWO,** the driver already in lane for his intended direction will normally take priority; the driver requiring to merge into that lane will

GIVE WAY if necessary. Thus at **D**, driver **B** will wait for **C** unless he cannot go easily ahead without **C** having to slow down. But before that, what happens to **B** at **A**? **U** and **B** *both* want to change lanes in opposite directions simultaneously! As **U** have your nose ahead of **B** he should let **U** go *but don't count on it.* If he looks like cutting ahead avoid a "battle". Scrapes and higher insurance rates are the usual results. Guilt may be impossible to prove and, besides, a Test examiner would take a poor view of an aggressive candidate.

However, take a lower gear while **U** assess what **B** will do. Then as soon as he slows, if he does, you can – provided there are no 2-wheelers squeezing up between the two of you *and traffic ahead isn't stopping* – accelerate to nip in front without delay. If **U** have to slow up and cross over behind **B** instead, the lower gear makes that easy too. But remember that by then your mirrors may be telling you to wait for more traffic from behind **B** first . . .

Very often in a one-way street a chance arises to change lane long before you need to do so.

Grab it.

Then you will avoid the possibility of any hold-up later.

On the other hand don't panic about changing lane and insist on trying to do it far too early. If your turning off the one-way is still half-a-mile away, that can cause an unnecessary delay too. Stay in the lane you are in and keep your eyes "open". An opportunity to merge over safely as you all flow along will almost certainly arise in good time, encouraged by your giving a signal extra early.

As you merge towards either edge of a one-way be particularly careful about roads entering from that side, whichever it is. People arriving to join the one-way *often* fail to look beyond the lane nearest to them. They don't expect you to be swooping across from a lane further away . . . In the opposite situation make sure you don't make that same error!

Occasionally you will come across a much wider one-way than depicted in fig. 72, and which arrives as the stem of a T at a multi-lane major road or dual carriageway with, say, two, or three, lanes each way. At the end of the one-way as many as 4 lanes may be available. There would probably be a traffic light to control the extra volume of traffic you would expect to find at such a spot.

In this type of place left or right exits from the one-way are often made from two lanes both moving side by side. Drivers enter the two appropriate lanes of the major road parallel and alongside each other when the lights turn in their favour. Therefore you may *not need* to get to the lefthand-most (or righthand-most) lane in advance. You can make your turn in a next-door lane and review which lane you want to continue in later, after joining the main road. This double-laned entry to the major road allows a bigger volume of traffic to exit the one-way at each light change.

The same thing sometimes happens at wide two-way traffic lights. Be on the look out for it.

U, *in fig. 73, are having to cross the one-way street to reach road* **B**. Imagine that heavy traffic in the one-way is here at a near-standstill, though individual lanes open up and move from time to time. You have to wait for a gap in the nearest lane so that you can move out, switching to left indicator as you do so. From there your line should be more or less direct as arrowed but, because of the traffic, the operation is almost certain to have to be stop-go as the breaks in the line show. It depends on how many lanes of traffic are flowing, their speed, and how easily one can merge over. Although drivers will often wait for you, you must avoid forcing anyone to have to brake or slow, or you could be failed for being insufficiently careful. In your haste to go when someone waits, never forget to look forward **WHERE YOU ARE GOING**. Vehicles there may still be STOPPED!

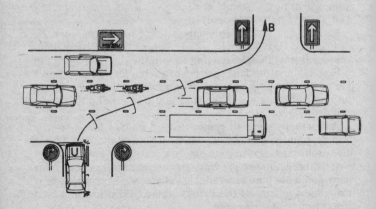

Fig. 73   Crossing a one-way street in stages.

AN L-DRIVER'S NIGHTMARE?

Look at fig. 74. Not really a nightmare but it is worth studying a big junction like this if you can, either on foot or as a passenger. You will gain useful insight for the day you arrive at one at the wheel. **U** must be careful to watch your traffic light **B** and not, say, **D**, because that activates the crossing traffic from **H**. You can cause an accident by starting to move on the wrong lights. It happens easily.

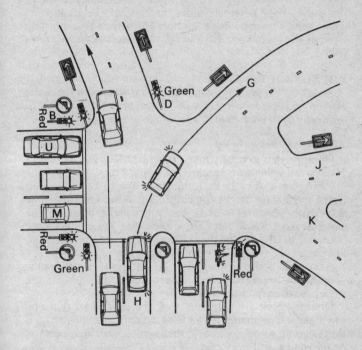

Fig. 74   An L-driver's nightmare?

If **U** are going to **K**, you ought to be where **M** is, but, though wrongly positioned, you may still be lucky and be able to ease across if there is no one behind you correctly laned for roads **G** or **J**. Otherwise you may have to go to **G** yourself and accept that as a penalty for being in the wrong lane.

ROUNDABOUTS

Roundabouts are clockwise one-way systems devised to smooth the safe interchange of traffic from several roads at once. At the majority of them you are going to find more than one lane on each approach road and several lanes around the roundabout too. Much of what I have to say is therefore concerned with **Lane Discipline** and is written with these bigger roundabouts in mind. The roundabout rules themselves, apply equally to smaller roundabouts where there may only be single lanes, and to MINI-roundabouts which (apart from having their own type of advance warning signs as shown in your Highway Code) are just smaller ones still.

ROUNDABOUTS' SYSTEM

The first rule of all roundabouts is that when you reach the broken line across your entry point, you *must* GIVE WAY *to the traffic from your right.*

Arrival

On approach normally take 3rd gear, and soon thereafter 2nd, as you slow down prepared to stop.

(Only for a very large roundabout where there was no traffic to be seen, might you consider that 3rd gear would be sufficiently powerful to make your entry and exit safely. The circumstances would have to be such that you could see no potential need for a further change down, and certainly no likelihood of having to stop at any stage.)

Arm signals are not appropriate at roundabouts unless your indicators have failed. You need both hands on the wheel. So use your indicators.

Double-check your mirrors *well* beforehand so that you can make a lane change *SEPARATELY, before you arrive,* if that is going to be necessary; then signal, and then *position on the road* as follows:

1) For the first exit left, in the lefthand lane, indicating left.

2) For an exit that is more straight on than it is to the right, in either the lefthand or the righthand lane, taking account of the weight of traffic approaching with you, or on the roundabout. Don't signal yet – other than for changing lane beforehand if that is appropriate. If there are more than two approach lanes a lefthand or middle one would probably be preferable.

3) For an exit that is more to the right than it is straight on,

in the righthand-most lane, signalling right.

As you come up gently to the line in 2nd gear, you must be weighing up whether you can go on without a stop, or will need to GIVE WAY to anyone from your right. If someone is in front of you, you also need to anticipate whether he will stop anyway, even if all is clear! Although the object is to keep going if you can – so as to keep traffic flowing – lots don't. You don't want to biff him in the boot while you are still too busy looking towards your right for traffic coming around the roundabout . . . And remember as well, that before you can enter the roundabout, there may be pedestrians crossing the neck of your road – *especially if another lane next to you is stopped*. Look out for them specifically.

Entry

To reach **A**, in fig. 75, **U** have to consider car **B**. Unless you can clear across **B's** route comfortably ahead of him in time, so that he could not possibly need to slow down, **U** must GIVE WAY to **B**. It certainly looks as if you would have to here! If **U** wait for **B** you still cannot then go without checking that **C** has begun his left indicator and that his front wheels confirm he is not going on round, or watching **D** who may by then have pulled out.

You don't only need to watch out for cars **B**, **C** and **D**. Your eyes must sweep *all* the tarmac to your right. You must move your head about too, to allow for the roof-pillar blind spot in front of your eyes. What about the pedal cyclist – to whom you must GIVE WAY – that I have shown spinning around the outside edge of the roundabout? *He will be crushed if your neck and eyes are lazy.* What about other riders to your right or to your left sweeping up alongside you from behind? You saw *them*, didn't you? As ever, yield to riders. They are exceptionally vulnerable at roundabouts.

If all is clear for you to carry on onto the roundabout, being in 2nd gear now allows you to do so without risk of stalling. If you have to stop then 1st gear will be needed for a **Smooth Start** in due course.

Don't get over-excited the instant you see a gap to tail on into. **LOOK FIRST WHERE YOU ARE ABOUT TO GO.** Traffic there could have stopped in front of your nose! You must double-check, too, for pedestrians crossing from your left or right and for riders who may by now have crept up alongside from behind. Only then can you go if safe and there is still plenty of time before you would have to GIVE WAY

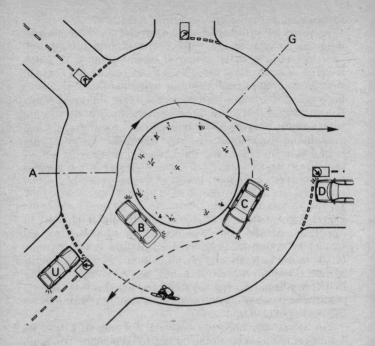

Fig. 75 Roundabout priorities.

to anyone new from your right.

Going Round

Think in lanes. Stay strictly in lane round the roundabout *even if no divisions are marked*.

1) For the first exit left keep to the lefthand, outer, roundabout lane, only.

2) For straight-on exits it is best to stay in the lane you chose on *Arrival* and *Entry*. Should you want to change lanes as you travel round the first one-third of the roundabout (i.e. well before your exit), you must only do so just as you would on any straight road. That is, giving ample warning, and GIVING WAY to anyone already in the lane to which you want to move.

3) For a righthand exit, take the righthand-most lane, "hugging" the roundabout edge all the way as you go round.

Exiting

1) A first-left exit should cause no problems. Always take a flash-look over your left shoulder just before turning into your exit road to make sure you won't squash any cyclist. Enter your new road in the left lane if there is more than one. Accelerate promptly unless traffic prevents you. Watch your mirrors at once; fast drivers/riders often take this opportunity to overtake if there is an outside lane or room available. Check that your indicator cancels.

2) For straight-on exits *from the lefthand lane,* begin signalling left as you pass the entry point last before your exit. Continue as in 1) above. Look out! – *before* you reach that *previous* entry/exit, someone from a middle or a righthand lane may swoop across in front of your nose to take it! Seeing you in the lefthand lane they could mistakenly expect you to be taking it too. Fault might be hard to apportion. Should you have given way to that driver as having come (basically) from your right (on a roundabout), or should he have waited for you before crossing your lane? My guess would be the former, at least unless he hit the rear half of your car, i.e. you were clearly well ahead in the first place. The Highway Code stipulates that you look out for exactly the likes of him.

For straight-on exits *from a middle or a righthand lane* you face the opposite dilemma. You begin signalling left at much the same stage or perhaps a fraction earlier – but not so soon anyone could imagine you were taking the previous exit. Although it probably would be your priority, you must now be prepared to allow anyone then in a lane left of yours to enter the new road first. Or, of course, to swing on round the roundabout to a later exit! Such a driver could have popped out from the previous exit itself, or may have zoomed round and caught you up from somewhere to your rear. Don't swerve about; just slow – keeping going round in your original lane for the time being – or pull up calmly if you need to. OR – and this may be easier and safer than stopping – just go all the way round again yourself. (You should never *reverse* if you have gone too far; just go round and try again.)

Note that you *may* be able to enter your road, if it has room, parallel with someone on your left, provided *you are certain* that that is where they are going.

Again, look to your mirrors and your indicator cancellation as soon as you are into the new road. Pick up speed promptly unless a traffic jam or good reason is stopping you.

3) For a righthand exit hug the roundabout edge until you are in line to leave – when U reach G in fig. 75. At that stage, or maybe a fraction earlier as just explained, you switch your righthand indicator, which, you will recall, should have been on all the time, to signal left. Continue exactly as in the 2nd, 3rd and 4th paragraphs of 2) just above.

The dilemma described above, where other lanes need to be crossed, plus the fact that traffic frequently grinds to a halt (or even stops suddenly) on a roundabout, mean your eyes must be "everywhere": mainly to the right and to the front on approach but in your mirrors too; ahead all the way round (and forward into the exit you want); with added quick flash-looks across your shoulders as required to augment your mirrors.

The huge, multi-laned, roundabouts in some cities and at trunk route intersections can "fool you as quick as look at you" at busy times. Give yourself *extra* time on approach. Go slow, while you sort out where you believe everyone to your right may be heading. If you have a doubt about a single vehicle in relation to where you intend to drive, don't enter the roundabout. Wait. See where he *does go*, first. Drivers of the race-circuit mentality wing round these lanes and off to their destinations very fast. Good judgment of how quickly they can be upon you will, I can assure you from my experiences of Learners, take much longer to acquire than you expect.

Remember that your good positioning and your correct speed will, almost by themselves, tell others where you are going. Make sure they are telling the right story.

Remember to treat any roundabout as a box junction. See **More To Watch Out For At Traffic Lights** earlier. If your route out of a roundabout is blocked, that really is no excuse for sitting strangling an entry point for others, when drivers there could perfectly easily make their way to different (open) exits if only you had left them room.

MULTIPLE ADJACENT ROUNDABOUTS

At a few places more than one roundabout has been built so that they can work in conjunction with one another. Sometimes two or three interrelate. These systems usually include some points where traffic *on a particular roundabout* has to GIVE WAY to traffic *entering* that roundabout (the reverse of the normal first rule of roundabouts I gave you). GIVE WAY lines across the roundabout lanes will be clearly marked. Be ready to wait if you have to.

"ROUND-THE-BLOCK" ROUNDABOUTS

You will find huge one-way systems round buildings or whole blocks; in effect they are vast roundabouts. For these systems simply combine the lane choice principles of round-abouts, with the lane use and lane change principles of ONE-WAYS given earlier.

NASTY SNAGS AT MINI-ROUNDABOUTS

Imagine you are going to go straight on at a mini-roundabout and that someone coming in the other direction, giving no signal, appears to be going to do the same from directly opposite you. There is no one else around. Without warning he swings round across in front of you to turn right! It can give you a fright suddenly to realise you have to GIVE WAY. The important thing is to assume nothing, till you see from his wheels that that driver *will* be going straight on – especially if he is going slowly enough to make a sudden turn instead.

Space may be so tight at a mini-roundabout that one or more of your wheels has to mount the painted mound itself. That's fine but don't allow the lack of room to be an excuse for cutting brazenly across!

On Test an examiner won't mind if you can't merge over to a lane you need on roundabout, but could fail you for a stupid or panic action. Panic normally proves inexperience. So do get sufficient roundabout practice.

UNMARKED CROSSROADS

These are surprisingly common in residential side streets and in country districts. The safe rule, whichever way you are going, including straight across, is to stop, or practically do so, before going on if it is safe. You have to imagine where GIVE WAY or STOP lines would have been painted had they been there. If it is blind in any direction, listen, and hoot too, before you go. But be ready to GIVE WAY *to all, unless they clearly stop for you.*

MULTIPLE CROSSROADS

Study fig. 76. U must watch that vanman **K** doesn't sail out not realising you are coming. Incredible, but it happens. With the buildings and being a van with poor side vision, his view is restricted. *Your* vision is also restricted, so *YOU* must slow lest someone appears.

K is danger man again if he mistakenly thinks **F** (who intends going down the main road) wants his road. Gaily roaring out he comes face to face with **F** and *crash!*

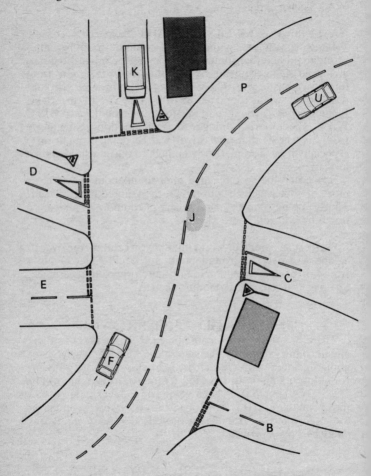

Fig. 76 A multiple crossroad.

If **K** wanted to go right to **D**, he would have to reach **J** when safe, making a proper turn from there when clear. *He must not cut straight over.* If he wanted road **E**, he would delay signalling till after **J**, in order to make his intention 100% clear.

Similarly if **U** are going right you should signal normally for **K's** road but wait for the correct moment for **D** or **E**.

To go left from **D** down the major road, you would signal left while waiting in **D**; you would cancel the signal at the instant of setting off, and steer directly down the major road towards **P**, so that anyone like **K** should be hard pressed to misinterpret you where you aim to go. But you still keep an eye in case they do misunderstand!

PART FOUR

BAD WEATHER – NIGHT DRIVING
AUTOMATICS – FRIGHTS – SKIDS
MOTORWAYS – QUESTIONS – YOUR TEST

BAD WEATHER

FOG AND POOR VISIBILITY

As a Learner avoid thick fog. When qualified do the same. Even the finest drivers can get caught up in the most terrible accidents being knocked on from behind. Fog tires your eyes and brain faster than most people expect. And it seems to fool them too. So why risk being out in it? Consider a hotel if you are far from home. If you must go out my advice is to stay off the fast-trafficked duals and bigger roads, where the dreadful pile-ups tend to occur.

IN FOG DO NOT DRIVE AT A SPEED FROM WHICH YOU CANNOT STOP WITHIN THE DISTANCE YOU CAN **STILL SEE** IS CLEAR **FROM MOMENT TO MOMENT**.

Nearly as important as seeing is to be seen. That is why the law requires you in fog to put on your headlamps (or sidelights together with paired fog lamps) whether in daylight or in darkness. (If you have front fog lamps it would be better to use them in conjunction with your *head*lamps.) Add your rear fog lamp(s) too.

This headlamps law extends beyond fog. You must do the same in any *seriously* reduced daytime visibility as defined in your Highway Code. I would include in that definition any dark squally patches, teeming rain, hail or snowfall. However, be careful not to leave rear fog lamps on when the need has passed. They are piercing, dazzling lights, especially at night, and cause dangerous eye-fatigue to others when

178

used unnecessarily. Make sure you know which setting of the switch is "ON" and what the dashboard reminder light looks like, so that you cannot join the hundreds who don't seem to understand their cars.

Day or night in fog have your headlamps on dipped beam. See NIGHT DRIVING next. High Beam in fog restricts vision rather than helps.

Be sure your windscreen isn't steamed inside. Wipe it initially with a clean rag till your de-mist arrangements, which need to be running at full *hot* blast, can keep it clear. In damp fog use windscreen wipers frequently – continuously if necessary. You will have enough problems coping with the fog without unwittingly adding more either side of the windscreen; so keep an eye that it remains clear all the time.

Maximum sane speed in fog may be walking pace or less. Satisfy your conscience that your speed is safe. It takes will power not to be tempted to keep with the man who whizzes past. He may have superb eyes, or lights; more likely is that he is one of those born every minute. Idiotic "following the lights" ends in countless multiple crashes.

Often the only way in fog is to crawl near the pavement edge, or the verge, using whichever is there as your guide. Range your eyes ahead, around – and up for traffic lights. Over-concentrating on the kerb could find you past red before your brain registers.

It can be bewildering, especially at night, to run *suddenly* into an unexpected patch of fog. It is frightening at speed but, unfortunately, it is on the very roads through open low country where speed tends to be higher that infrequent patches are most common. If it happens slow up at once – stop if necessary. Get your headlamps on fast. **NEVER** speed on, hoping the patch will be small. If you know there is fog in the air, drive slower, particularly on a strange road. And when you see a fog patch ahead slacken speed to a safe level *before reaching it*. To risk panic stations by running into a wall of fog too fast is madness. When you go on motorways after your Test remember that they are particularly prone to having patchy fog.

CLOUDBURSTS
Use dipped headlamps day or night during the worst of such conditions, to comply with the law, *to be seen*.

FIRST SPITS OF RAIN

Wipers used on too dry a screen can scratch it, as gritty dust and dirt is carried across. The wiper blades get damaged too. But more important is the way your entire view can disappear during the first few sweeps of the screen, as the grease and dirt spread out into an opaque blinding film before your very eyes!

In that event *slow or stop at once* until your windscreen washer can clear enough for you to see. Pull in if necessary. Sometimes switching off the wipers for a moment lets the greasy film "evaporate" offering temporary respite.

Always look at the road, not the smears on the screen.

Taking preventative measures, however, is more sensible than being caught out. Keep your windscreen, the wiper blades and your bonnet area clean. When you switch on your wipers for the first time on a journey always pick a safe moment from the traffic point of view. Let some rainwater build up before you switch on, and squirt the washers too, to help wash the screen as fast as possible. Carry a soapy sponge so that you can always stop, get out, and sort things out properly if necessary. Never be too lazy to do that.

NIGHT DRIVING

As an advanced Learner you will want to gain extra practice at night even though the Test is in daylight.

After dark (from the tick of lighting up time) it is illegal to drive without headlamps on unless, in a built up area, there are streetlamps alight less than 185 metres apart. Sidelights are obligatory even then but, frankly, the lamp-post test is a technicality you can ignore. The sensible thing is to have headlamps on at all official night times anyway, wherever you are, so that you will be seen as well as able yourself to see. In towns (where a few drivers seem to believe headlamps are somehow not needed) people leaving side-streets take a quick look and pull out; they shouldn't but they do. In their too hasty glance they miss tiny sidelights especially if their attention is momentarily diverted to a vehicle *using headlamps*, further behind you.

Headlamps also save pedestrians.

The 185 metre rule does not apply to out-of-town trunk roads or to motorways where either are lit. Headlamps must be on all night on them.

Use sidelights for up to half an hour *before* lighting up time and similarly after the dawn.

WHICH BEAM?

In **PART ONE** you should have learnt to find and use the headlamp on/off switch and the dipswitch by touch and feel. Did you also spot the (usually) blue dashboard warning light which, when your headlamps are on, tells you whether or not they are on High Beam penetrating their furthest? You must be able to recognize that warning light before you can drive safely at night, so that you can be certain that you are on dipped beam whenever that is necessary.

1) At all times when you have someone ahead *in front of you*, you MUST drive on dipped headlamps.

This prevents dazzling him by the reflection of your lights in his mirrors. Drop further behind than usual if you feel that your headlamps are still causing him difficulty.

If you are dazzled from behind use the anti-dazzle position of your interior mirror. However it is better in my view, unless you have especially sensitive eyes, not to switch to that setting permanently. It distorts and reduces what you see. I prefer to offset the mirror a little and retain a truer picture. Avoid letting your eyes become fixed in any of your mirrors. If you do get temporarily blinded slow down until your eyes readjust.

2) With nothing ahead of you High Beam is *essential to see properly*. However, it MUST only be used when there is no oncoming traffic – the humble bicycle included.

3) *Whenever someone is coming – dip,* returning to High Beam immediately he has passed if no others appear.

You can often prepare to dip before the headlamps of an oncoming vehicle themselves appear in the distance. You see when you will have to do so, judging by the light beams shining up ahead of the vehicle, perhaps up over a brow or around a corner as you both approach it from opposite directions.

4) Always dip while turning at junctions.

For safe night driving everyone ought to learn proper use of headlamps. Slower drivers often find traffic streams build up behind them at night. The many lazy (or perhaps fearful) ones who don't bother with High Beam but drive permanently dipped, then make overtaking them much harder. This is particularly so out in the country. Safe opportunities are missed because those behind are restricted in long-range vision to the length of the slower driver's dipped beam. Resulting impatience often means hazardous risks are taken.

5) So help those who want to pass, by using High Beam whenever you should. Dip as they go by until they are well clear.

SPEED IN THE DARK

NEVER BE TEMPTED TO DRIVE AT A SPEED FROM WHICH YOU CANNOT STOP WITHIN THE DISTANCE YOUR HEADLAMPS SHOW TO BE CLEAR. **NEVER ONCE.**

Maximum safe speeds on High Beam will be slower than in the day, and on dipped beam considerably slower.

If you are dazzled by oncoming traffic you *must* slow or stop till *you* can see. Don't take risks or blame others; *you* are responsible for your driving.

You can reduce dazzle, by averting your eyes away from approaching headlamp beams and concentrating mainly on seeing your own side of the road properly. It is no good allowing yourself to be "hypnotized" by the lights of the oncomer; that prevents you from seeing pedestrians, cyclists or obstructions on your own side.

If an approaching driver has forgotten to dip, a *brief* up-flash of your lights should remind him. But, of course, deliberately to dazzle back would be stupid, only increasing danger.

NIGHT TIPS

In country night driving, flashing your lights up and down even if there is no apparent oncoming traffic, announces your presence at hazards, for example, approaching a bend, junction, hump-back bridge or a hill top. *In the seconds you are dipped you see approaching light beams easily. In the seconds you are on High Beam others see yours.*

Keep your headlamps efficient. It is crazy and illegal to drive with just one headlamp or just one spot lamp. People coming the other way can mistake you for a motorcycle until it is too late! There's little point in lighting up dirt on the outside of your headlamps! Keep a damp sponge to wipe them over at least every time you stop for fuel. Use it more often if the car doesn't have a headlamp wash/wipe feature. Take that opportunity to wipe over all your other lamps, front and back, too. It only takes seconds and may save your life or someone else's.

Never reverse at night unless you must. If you do, putting on your hazard warning lamps helps you to see, as does flicking your brakelights on specially from time to time with your brake pedal. Both tips improve the poor vision a reversing light gives and, perhaps even more important, they help alert someone suddenly coming on the scene as to what is happening.

If you ever need to wait at the kerbside for a few moments in the dark be sure your headlamps are off. Headlamps on, on a stationary vehicle at the roadside at night – especially if they are on High Beam – are very off-putting to drivers.

AUTOMATIC TRANSMISSION

I remind you that a Test pass with automatic transmission restricts you to this type of vehicle only.

ONLY THE RIGHT FOOT

To drive an automatic USE ONLY YOUR RIGHT FOOT, NEVER THE LEFT. There are only two pedals with which to cope. You move your right foot from the accelerator on the right to the brake on the left, and back, as required.

Don't listen to those who claim you can brake with the left foot. It can only lead to muddle and the danger, in emergency, of finding yourself accelerating against your brakes.

THE SELECTOR LEVER

With the majority of automatic transmissions there are four basic positions of the selector lever. They are *Park, Reverse, Neutral* and *Drive*. One or more numbered gear *Lock* positions is/are also provided.

Park This provides a safety hold on the transmission preventing the car running away should the handbrake fail when parked. Use it only when parked. You should never engage it during driving.

Reverse Delicate control can be achieved for manoeuvring. In *Reverse*, handbrake off, the car can be held by the footbrake (right foot) and moved smoothly at a mile-an-hour simply by releasing the pressure of the right foot on the brake. For increased reverse speed accelerate *gently*, as required, returning the right foot to the brake to stop. Use a featherlight touch on the accelerator to prevent ever giving too much at once. In manoeuvring, the car can be held by the footbrake while the selector is moved from *Drive* to *Reverse* or vice-versa.

Neutral In *Neutral* the gears are disengaged. For safety, on most makes, it is only possible to start the engine with the lever in *Neutral* or in *Park*. Otherwise the car could shoot off on the starter. So the procedure if the car stalls is quickly to hold the car on your footbrake while you get the lever back into *Neutral* FAST. That then enables you to restart the engine and re-select *Drive* (or *Reverse*) to get you moving again. *It is a process you must practise many times, so that you can do it almost without conscious thought should you ever need it in a hurry.*

Drive In *Drive* (the normal driving position) gear changes *look after themselves.* When you select *Drive* before moving off, the gearbox automatically engages 1st; as you accelerate, it changes itself to 2nd directly the proper speed is reached and so on. Likewise downward changes are made as you slow down.

All you need to grasp is the correct procedure for moving off. Here that is. I assume you are sitting with the handbrake on and the engine started, with the selector still in *Park* or *Neutral*, ready to begin:

(1) Apply the footbrake *using your right foot.*

(2) Move the selector to *Drive*; release the handbrake.

(3) Check your mirrors and, accordingly, signal when the moment to go appears ripe.

(4) Continue holding the car with the footbrake while you make your final checks that it is safe to move off.

(5) When safe change the right foot from the brake to the accelerator and gently squeeze it till you build up the speed required.

To slow down you simply release your accelerator to begin with. Add braking if and when required *using the right foot*: the gears, of course, change down automatically. When stopping come to a stop on the footbrake.

Never normally select *Drive* or release your handbrake in the above sequence till you have the car secure on the footbrake. On a hill it could run forward (or even back) before you are ready. More important, *Drive* could take the car forward against the handbrake, especially if the automatic or the manual choke on a cold engine was causing a high engine tick-over speed.

Lock 1, 2 etc. These selector lever positions enable you to override the automatic upward gear changes and keep in a low gear. This may be important for overtaking, to prevent the gear box changing up before you want it to, or for keeping in a low gear to achieve engine braking.

A simple standard automatic transmission has three gears within *Drive*, and *Lock 1* and *2*, i.e. on 1st and 2nd gear. However, you can find there are more gears and additional options. Therefore I must ask you to discuss with your teacher before you start, the precise details of the set-up on your car. Improvements to automatic transmissions are being developed all the time, and new transmissions are being introduced which work on entirely different principles.

Space here precludes discussing all the variations. Therefore I continue my notes based on a simple standard three gear unit.

KICKDOWN

For rapid acceleration a "kickdown" gear change facility is provided. This operates when the gear selector is in *Drive* or is in *Lock 2*. It can be used from rest or from any speed up to the maximum in 2nd gear (in the three gear automatic). Above that speed, naturally, it can't apply. On pressing the accelerator fully to the floor *and holding it there*, the gears change down. Depending on speed this will be to 1st (if not already in 1st), or to 2nd if speed is too high for 1st anyway (unless already in 2nd). The gear box thereafter only changes up as the maximum in each gear is reached (but only as far as 2nd if you are in *Lock 2*), thus providing the quickest possible acceleration. Release your accelerator pedal pressure at any time and the gears immediately change up (unless already in 2nd, in *Lock 2*), speed levelling off. Top kickdown speed varies but in some cars it is as high as 70 m.p.h.

Avoid using kickdown on skiddy surfaces. The slight jerk and temporary loss of power of such a forceful automatic gear change can be enough to trigger a skid.

HINTS AND PITFALLS

For moving off uphill use the normal procedure explained above. *For steep hills only* (more than say 15%), you may need to alter the procedure slightly, and instead of holding the car only on the footbrake from (2), keep the handbrake on till (4). While you are checking that all is safe during (4), switch your right foot to giving *slight* acceleration – till you feel the car straining to go. For (5) you can now release the

185

handbrake, increase the acceleration and away you go! *Never* allow your handbrake to get slack. Otherwise, as you may guess, steep uphill starts can cause problems!

In stop-start traffic you can hold the car on the footbrake at each stop. Stay in *Drive*. Simply switch your foot to the accelerator when ready to go. (You might need to add your handbrake – as above – on a very steep uphill.)

However, when stopped for any long period it is better driving to *use your handbrake* and return to *Neutral*. Then you can take your foot off the footbrake and relax. As a bonus your brake lights are thereby extinguished which saves eye-strain for people behind, particularly when it is wet or dark.

It is also safer driving to use your handbrake *and* come back to *Neutral* whenever you stop for long *at the front*, at traffic lights, other junctions, zebra crossings and wherever pedestrians wander across in front of you. The habit safeguards you against mistakes and calamities. Suppose you are the first to stop, say, at a Pelican crossing. Dreaming for a moment, your foot crosses to the accelerator and squeezes it. If you were still in *Drive* . . . Equally, suppose an attack of cramp made you powerless to prevent ramming on the accelerator? Form good habits from the outset.

If you get stuck in the mud or on ice or snow, you may be able to extract the car by selecting *Reverse* and then *Drive* alternately – whilst using no accelerator at all. A second or two in each gear in quick succession, rocks the car to the stage where (hopefully) you climb away from the sticking point.

FRIGHTS

BURST TYRES, PUNCTURES

With a puncture you usually get warnings, e.g. heavy steering, bumpier ride, wandering, general worsening unbalance. If you feel something is wrong, or firm (or light) braking makes you swerve, check ALL your tyres straight-away.

A burst (blow out) is rare. If it happens you may hear the bang and hiss, or, if you have hit something, expect it, but possibly your first warning will be a sudden feeling of reduced control as the car tries to veer.

Act: Never panic. Grip the steering wheel tightly. Keep the

car straight unless you have to steer to get past immediate danger. Light your hazard warning lamps. Aim to slow and stop with the least possible braking, to avoid further unbalancing the car. Should the car swerve anyway you may have to battle with the steering to avoid hitting anything or going over a precipice! Once your speed is right down swop your hazard lamps to left indicator and pull off the road if you possibly can. See the breakdown emergency waiting advice in your Highway Code.

If your tyres are good and you avoid hitting kerbs at speed you may never have a burst. Never drive fast on old worn tyres – especially if they do not have a suitable ply rating for higher speeds. Check that with your tyre suppliers – and that none of your tyres is yet illegal to use!

RUNNING OUT OF PETROL/
ACCELERATOR CABLE BREAK

The engine splutters and fails or power suddenly dies.

Act: Directly you realise your engine is conking out get your clutch pedal down. This will enable you to coast (freewheel) a little further and, hopefully, to get the car off the road into a safe position. If you haven't just committed to memory the emergency breakdown advice in your Highway Code (as above) please do it now! Wise drivers never travel on a nearly empty tank.

WINDSCREEN SHATTERS

Act: Stop as soon as you safely can. Get off the road before some idiot hits you. A clear zone is normally built in, which should allow you time to do that. My advice then is to telephone and have the screen replaced immediately. Screen specialists are everywhere. To attempt to travel on looking through a bashed-out hole, can only be regarded as dangerous to others on the road and because fine particles of glass can so easily be flipped into your eyes.

STALLING

Act: Stop and hold the car on your footbrake, bring on your handbrake and return to *Neutral*. Re-start quickly so you can then move yourself out of danger. Make sure you are in the right gear this time if that has been the problem.

As a "life-saver" if about to be hit but can't start, for example to get your car off a level crossing, move on the starter in gear. The strength of the battery and starter motor should get you clear and off the road. Use 2nd or 3rd gear (or reverse if appropriate), clutch up.

Unfortunately you cannot employ this last resort with automatic transmission.

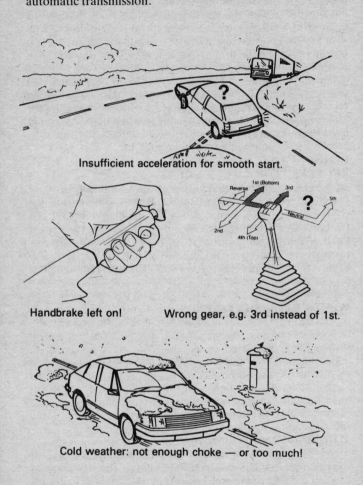

Insufficient acceleration for smooth start.

Handbrake left on!   Wrong gear, e.g. 3rd instead of 1st.

Cold weather: not enough choke — or too much!

Fig. 77 Common causes of stalling.

Stalling is the cause of many grave accidents at junctions. To avoid being a victim take note of figs. 53 and 77.

BRAKE FAILURE

Rare – but it happens.

Act: Don't lose a second. Try your handbrake. It can only produce a fraction of the stopping power of your footbrake but that fraction is worth having. Also "smash" to a lower gear, 4th to 3rd, then to 2nd and to 1st, letting the engine slow you down. Switch on your headlamps; sound your horn continuously rapid-fire – beep, long beep, long beep, fashion. At least you are then giving some warning to other people. With luck you may be able to squeeze through safe gaps until you come to a stop. Last resorts could be mounting an empty pavement and grazing a side of the car against the wall; or perhaps going through a hedge into a field. Avoid the head-on killer crash. Miss all you can rather than hit soft, human, flesh, or anything hard like concrete.

BREAKDOWN

If you break down on a fast-trafficked road don't just sit there! Put on hazard warning lights at once. Try to push the car or drive it on the starter as under **Stalling** a few paragraphs back, onto the verge if there is one. Follow the breakdown Highway Code advice you have just learned properly (see above!). An open boot lid with a back seat squab or a spare wheel leaned up against your back bumper is a universally recognized sign that you can make to warn people coming up from behind of your trouble. An open bonnet alerts people from ahead. Use a warning triangle and/or cones as well if you can.

FAST DRIVING

Driving generally too fast for your personal ability to cope safely, creates emergencies and leads to terrible frights. Skids, crashes, and death or tragic injury for innocent people, are the inevitable results.

Nevertheless driving fast and hitting the best average speeds genuinely within your capability can be safe.

The first necessity is the *self discipline* constantly to match speed to conditions, never exceeding the maximum speed for safety *even when that is one mile per hour*. The hall-mark of the **SAFE** fast driver – and it's no paradox – is actually his *slowness*, his almost obsessional slowness in potential danger where others rush on without thought. You may not see him for dust otherwise but that is the feature that consistently marks him out from the fast fool.

The second prerequisite is skill, built step-by-step through experience. Until you have several 100,000 miles behind you don't even consider fast driving. You are still a babe in knowhow. Many young-bloods die because they won't accept this. Seventeen to at least the late twenties are the dangerous years – just the years when most cannot, on account of their age, have the mileage behind them.

The third indispensable requirement is fitness. This must include first-class eyesight, hearing and speed of reactions. Lack of stress is vital too. Never allow irritability, tiredness, illness or temporary discomfort (e.g. hunger, cold etc.) to influence your driving.

Finally your car must be *roadworthy for being driven fast*. Tremendous extra stresses and strains affect a car in fast driving. A car built for speed is quite different from many so-called sports cars or the ageing family banger. It is a precision machine maintained regardless of cost. Unless you have the right car in good condition, leave fast driving to others. Be willing to be restricted according to the quality of your car. If you have such a car as a brand new Ferrari, you have, of course, perhaps an even greater obligation to drive it in a manner fitting for the mark.

SKIDS

At least one third of all accidents involve skidding. Accidents blamed on skidding always arise from *lack of anticipation*. That poor anticipation results from *insufficient knowledge of skids, and of their prevention*, coupled with corresponding ignorant excessive speeds. Drivers go recklessly fast when space for manoeuvre is tight and, even worse, when road-surface conditions are also tricky – gambling that no emergency will ever happen.

Of course, one day, one will.

I pray that you will never join the ranks of those consumed by such idiocy.

Prevention [of skids] is far, far better than cure. Throughout my book I have tried to demonstrate how and where emergencies so easily happen. I have implored you to get speed down beforehand whenever potential danger closes in. Even so, you are bound to experience skids. Although, hopefully, they won't be too serious you must be able to recognize any type of skid instantly. Only if you can do that can you hope to react correctly at once.

I divide skids into three main types: those which happen *when you are braking hard* – those caused by *over-acceleration* – and those where speed or cornering is simply too fast and the car slides *sideways* off its course. I call the latter *sideslip* skids. This is a word of my own invention to encompass all front-wheel or 4-wheel skids of which the *main root* is excessive speed in the conditions, as distinct from skids which arise mainly through braking or over-acceleration.

Chart figs. 78, 80 and 81 in the next few pages, define each of these sorts of skids.

LOCKED BRAKES

In the above charts "locking", first mentioned in **PART ONE**, means when one or more road wheels *stop turning*, momentum (weight x speed) thereafter taking the car along with that (or those) wheel(s) sliding.

The first thing you must understand is that **WHILE THE FRONT BRAKES ARE LOCKED YOU CANNOT STEER.** There may be a loss of sideways control at the back too, as rear wheels slide, but in the charts, and in the explanatory text connected with each one, I will refer to this as such so as to prevent any confusion with the more fearsome *sideslip* skids above.

A wheel locks when its tyre "footprint" (the part in contact with the road at any moment) loses its grip. Under heavy braking, a huge transfer of the impact of the weight of the vehicle, suddenly bears down on the front wheels. You see the nose dive. It's not surprising therefore, that the hold against the road that that "footprint" on each front tyre can exert, has a limit which will be beaten eventually. Less obvious, perhaps, is that because weight is also *lifted off* the back wheels by the braking, they too will be more inclined to become skittish and slide.

The added momentum which results from going downhill causes this tyre adhesion to be broken sooner.

On the turn (for a corner), additional (wheels') rolling resistance and sideways weight re-distribution exacerbate the problems. This is why I originally pointed out early in **PART TWO**, under **Emergency Stop On Test**, that "locking" is less likely if you can keep the steering straight.

From excessively high speeds *on wet roads* "locking" sliding may change, at least until speed comes down a little, temporarily into locked-wheel *aquaplaning*. (See also page

206.) The already tenuous grip sliding provides, at least means some contact with the road is still existing. During such locked-wheel *aquaplaning* however, your tyres are each carried along on a wedge of water which is created because they are no longer turning and efficiently ejecting that water. They are completely out of touch with the road. For the steering wheels at least, this frightening phenomenon means you are a whole step further away from regaining control, even after you get your foot off the brake long enough to try to let them roll. This is because they can't even do that again until these wedges of water have dispersed sufficiently for contact with the road to be regained.

SKIDS WHEN BRAKING HARD
See chart fig. 78 first.

Prevention
   (a) avoiding mechanical defects
Never save pence per mile by using worn tyres. They skid lethally easily. A soft tyre may cause the car to wander, or to pull to one side when braking. Look at your tyres daily. Check air in them at least once a month; also check that tread depths/quality exceed the minimum legal limits. (See Question 43.)

Don't overload. This increases momentum and alters balance, making control more difficult, as does lopsided loading. Note that higher tyre pressures may be recommended for family holiday loading, etc. Take extreme care when loaded more than usual.

Always have well-adjusted brakes. Braking from higher speeds is hazardous even with perfect brakes because the car's momentum acts increasingly against you; if your brakes are poor or badly adjusted, which is rarely evident at lower speeds, this danger is disproportionately multiplied at high speed and therefore becomes deadly. Bad brakes or an under-inflated tyre (front or back) can unbalance the car, throwing it to one side at once whenever the brakes are applied. Any maladjustment or tyre fault must be put right immediately it has been noticed.

Keep an eye on your brake power. See pages 84 and 194. Remember brake linings easily wear through *between* long service intervals and that brake hydraulics can spring a leak at any time. See fig. 7 for warning symptom.
   (b) watching road causes

SKIES WHEN BRAKING HARD

Wheel(s) lock(s) up. Car slides forward: steering disappears during front-wheel "locking"; you may lose part of or all sideways control at the back too if/when a/the back wheel(s) lock(s). Results dramatically accentuated downhill. "Locking" is more likely if braking on a corner – which would be wrong anyway. Skidding likelihood greatly increased where there is an adverse camber (see fig. 79).

CONTRIBUTORY CAUSES

(a) mechanical defect
Bald tyre(s).
Tyres soft or over-inflated, slow puncture.
Front wheels (or back ones) not having matched tread pattern, *condition* or type (e.g. radial tyres mixed illegally with cross-ply ones – see Question 43).
Overloading, unbalanced load.
Wrongly adjusted brakes.
Poor suspension.
Other more technical defects.

(b) road cause
Wet surface.
Slippery surface (oil, etc.).
White lines (wet).
Cobbles (wet).
Loose surfaces (gravel, sticky leaves, mud etc.).
Uneven surface.
"Black" (invisible) ice/"freezing rain", ice/snow.
Adverse camber.
Bend.
Downhill.

(c) human error
Excessive brake pedal pressure by driver is main cause (perfect brakes will lock ultimately; when, merely depends on the road surface). Sudden instead of progressive braking.
Arriving at a bend too fast.
Sudden downward gear change made late, when going too fast.

Not making allowances for road causes, or not recognising and dealing with vehicle defects, inevitably precedes these skids.

Fig. 78 Skids when braking hard.

The problem of "locking" your brakes is multiplied many times on wet roads. That is why in my last paragraph under **The Gap To Leave** in **PART TWO**, I gave a rule-of-thumb – never to be broken – for wet roads. If you don't recall that rule now, please look at it again so that you can brand it into your mind.

Here is the exercise I promised you on page 70. It will enable you to recognise "locking" brakes and to ingrain correct reactions to them *in practice* as distinct from theory. Page 70 gave you the theory. Now you need a *wide, quiet* road with *no traffic*. Read that theory again. Then do some trials.

Work on a dry day first before trying on a wet day, preferably at the same place, and thus discovering the dramatic difference a little water can make . . . Each time start the trials with your teacher demonstrating before you try. Then you should know what to expect.

Without ever exceeding 20 m.p.h. practise fast stops using hard braking pedal pressure. Don't begin from any greater speed because that could be dangerous. Keep well away from the edge. Pay attention to your mirrors.

Doing these "emergency" stops you should find that the car halts after sliding in a reasonably straight line. (The amount of sliding and how quickly you stop will depend on how quickly you become adept at turning theory into practice – on how quick you are at working your brake off and back on at every hint of a wheel "locking".) Slight loss of steering control, or of sideways control at the back is allowable but any serious loss, provided the steering was straight, would probably be the result of a *mechanical defect* that needs looking into at once.

Practise at every lesson till you can confidently minimise stopping distances required, wet or dry.

Also try on a *downhill* stretch and see for yourself how much extra distance you need when going down. *Your speeds downhill must always allow for the huge increase to your momentum which is caused by a decline.* If you wish to try *uphill*, later, you will find conversely how a hill then helps you stop.

Plenty of other changes in road conditions can be treacherous. Some much more so than simple wetness. Transparent oiliness is one. On a film of unseen oil, "locking" can happen the instant you touch your brakes, even lightly. The time to be most alert is when rain begins to fall, especially after a long dry spell and at places like traffic lights where vehicles often queue. This is because oil drops left by traffic mix with the rain, and isolated patches soon spread into large areas of "ice-rink" conditions. Only after considerable heavy rain does this oiliness begin to be washed away.

Gravel, leaves, mud, cow dung etc. claim their victims because instead of gripping the road the tyres grip on the loose material on the surface. That material slides carrying you and your car with it!

Many white road markings are painted with a cement-based paint. In wet conditions especially, the grip on this may differ from that on the road. Avoid having to brake with a wheel(s) on them if you can as this may unbalance your braking.

The worst feature of black (invisible) ice is that all too often its presence will initially take you by surprise. In the deep winter months look out for it wherever a chill wind is able to tear across carriageways unprotected by high banks etc. If you see lorry drivers or other professionals going slowly take the hint: *black ice is a killer*.

Motor cyclists dragging one foot provide a clue you cannot ignore! The sight of a grit spreading lorry should too . . .

Nonetheless your first inkling that this ruthless agent of death is about, may be feeling a *sudden lightness in the steering*. Or, you may discover it by an unexpected over-acceleration skid (see chart fig. 80), or perhaps by finding instant "locking" of your brakes the moment you touch that pedal.

Immediately you are aware of being on black ice ease off your accelerator and slacken speed. Get right down to 15 m.p.h. or less as soon as you possibly can but:

Don't jam on your brakes and skid to kingdom come!

Then, with an eye to your mirrors, test your brakes *gently* from time to time to discover whether you have passed through the dangerous patch. Keep speed low even after that and keep checking carefully to see whether you have run into another sheet of invisible ice.

Sometimes black ice appears in a form termed by weather men as "freezing rain". This can be so glassy that driving may prove impossible. In such wintry conditions always carry warm clothing and have a full tank of petrol in case you are stuck in your car for a long time, and need to have the engine running for working your interior heater. Be prepared to leave the car in a safe position and walk to safety.

On snow 15 m.p.h. is enough. 20 m.p.h. is more than enough.

Where snow gets packed down and ice forms on top of it "locking" can occur instantly on braking. It can even happen to the front wheels when all you do is try to alter course!

For normal stopping on snow or ice use gentle braking. However, if the brakes are causing an immediate slide, the best way to stop on snow may be to go down the gears (no acceleration) until speed is almost zero in 1st – before trying to pull up finally on your footbrake; nevertheless, let the clutch up cautiously after each gear change as even a tiny jerk can be enough to induce a wheel-"locking" skid. By this method you may gain the benefit of some engine braking.

Important advice for stopping on snow is to pick your track onto virgin snow wherever you can. Even if you can only get one side of your car off the beaten track the overall grip you are getting should be improved. Although your wheels may lock nearly as quickly as on icy parts, the snow-plough effect, as they each have to push a quickly-mounting pile of snow, helps to stop you.

Approaching a downhill slope drop speed to almost nothing and get into low gear *before* you arrive. For a steep downhill 1st gear may be necessary. Thus you can venture down, only letting speed rise very little by very little, holding back as soon as you feel it is getting too high. Should you ever lose control downhill you may also have to take to the edge or jump the verge – pedestrians permitting – as your main hope.

You may worry that the car will stick through lack of speed. Don't worry! That is a damn sight safer than losing control.

You need to leave stopping distances on ice, black ice or snow and ice, of extraordinary length, many, many times more than normal. And further still if you are going downhill. You can only discover how long they should be, through *extra gentle* testing to see how slippery whatever you are on actually is, and assessing your stopping power fairly frequently in that way.

By far the best means to learn to handle your car in these conditions is to have your teacher, or some other long, long winter-experienced friend, show you the ropes before attempting it yourself. Apart from perhaps a few slow-motion experiments with your instructor, Learners should avoid snow or ice for a year or two after passing the Test.

Then it is worth taking advantage of some snowy weather for practising some deliberate minor skids, at slow speeds, in safe places, which will warn you of the terror of serious ones.

See fig. 79. All roads have an inbuilt camber. Their surface is curved in a convex fashion, the road centre-line always being constructed higher than the edges. If you could take a sectional view across at right angles to the road, you would see why rain-water will always drain away from the middle towards the gutters. On well-engineered roads this cambering effect is re-designed at sharper bends so that both sides of the centre-line slope the same way – into the inner angle of the corner. All rain-water flows that way as a result. More important the revised camber tends to help a car cornering too fast on the outside of the bend, to stay on the road. Where the engineers haven't cambered a road properly in this way at a bend, then what is known as *adverse* camber, far from helping, acts as a positive hindrance to vehicles sticking on the road. In Area **A** of the badly built road in fig. 79 the camber is wrong.

(c) <u>eliminating human error</u>

This depends upon *good* anticipation, which, in turn, can only grow through knowledge, experience, concentration, and above all, self-disciplined control of speed.

Such anticipation depends on knowledge in one further area – cornering.

WHEN YOU APPROACH A CORNER ALL NECESSARY BRAKING MUST BE COMPLETE BEFORE YOU REACH IT.

"Slow in *fast* out" at corners is an old racing-driving motto. "Slow in *drive* out" (not so fast) should generally be yours.

If you brake or are still braking once you begin to turn, like U have been doing in fig. 79, and your wheels slide (which, as explained, is more likely anyway when your steering wheels are not straight), several forces instantly gang up against you as well. Centrifugal force (remember spinning a conker on a string and letting it go?) tries to whirl you out off the bend. Momentum wants to take you straight on. Adverse camber, if any, speeds you on your skidding way. If you are going downhill all these problems are enormously accentuated.

If **U** arrive at a speed well over the top, as in fig. 79, the chances are you will skid straight on once you slide, whatever corrections you try to make. Even if you get your foot off the brake quickly enough to kill the initial straight-on skid and regain steering control, you may still be in trouble from the above trio of factors further round the corner, by then in the clutches of a deadly *sideslip* skid. *Sideslip* skids are considered separately in their own section shortly.

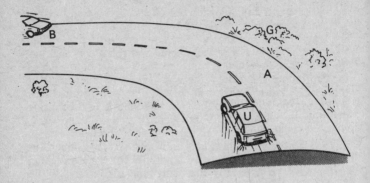

Fig. 79 Adverse camber

Therefore "Slow in" is crucial. But why "drive out"? The answer in non-technical terms is that your renewed forward traction helps to take you where you want to go. It counters the nose dive of braking and redistributes the weight more evenly between the four wheels as you go round.

You should begin re-accelerating lightly from a little *prior to the apex* of the corner, all slowing or braking (as stated above), having been completed before that.

When you take a bend correctly you can feel the car perky and squat on the road instead of lolling over towards the two outside wheels, as will happen if you arrive too fast and precariously close to overcooking it.

The "*drive* out" technique is as vital an element of safe cornering as is the "Slow in" routine. It is the *combination* of the two that should keep you well-balanced throughout every corner, safe. To have the one without the other, though better than nothing, can never be half so good.

In the context of avoiding skidding therefore, I stress completing all braking before a turn or a bend.

In the course of *normal smooth safe driving*, however, your aim should be always to time your approach so that *such braking is hardly required anyway*.

198

That's what good driving is all about.

You have to relate your reduction of speed to the sharpness of the corner. That reduction must be sufficient in all the circumstances of wet, snow, adverse camber, being downhill or whatever, to enable you then to "*drive* (through and) out", with only a light touch on your accelerator till you are in the straight again on your way.

You must never *over*-accelerate on the way round. That could cause an over-acceleration skid and more problems, about which see further below.

If the bend is sufficiently sharp to dictate a speed slow enough for 3rd or 2nd gear get down to that gear well before you arrive. It is important not to have to change gear on the way round. If you were anywhere near the limit of adhesion, doing that could unbalance your car, or even trigger a skid. Being in the right gear from beforehand enables you to take a bend properly, STEADILY under gentle constant power, and then pick up your former speed without delay directly you come out of it.

Get down those gears *smoothly* using the changing down refinement of my page 87. On a damp surface a bad match of engine revs to road speed as you changed could be all it needs to make your driving wheels lock, which – at the least – will cause a temporary skid till speed drops.

Correction

Correction of brake-induced skids rests mainly with quickness to spot the problem, getting your steering straight, and skill using the anti- wheels "locking" braking technique learned in the exercise a few pages back.

In extreme danger you may to save life have to give steering, priority over braking. (Remember that while your front wheels are "locking" you *cannot steer*. Only in the moments your foot is eased off the brake will you have a chance to steer.) Faced with having to save a human life or perhaps immediately to avoid certain destruction, steer for *the least dangerous course*. Bump the side of a stationary car rather than have a head-on smash, or mount a pavement if clear. Forced over a kerb to avert a disaster, hold the steering wheel tightly as you steer across it at a reasonably sharp, not a shallow, angle, or you risk glancing off, back into danger, and perhaps a greater chance of being overturned. Your wheels and tyres may be ruined but with luck you will be safe.

In fig. 79 U should have braked *harder earlier,* while on the straight. At this late stage, far too far out in the road, you would need to brake gingerly if at all, so that if the grip of your tyres were with luck to be strong enough, you would still get round without upsetting your balance. However, if you knew in your heart and bones that you weren't going to make it and **B** appeared, you might well need to choose the sacrifice of going – deliberately – through the hedge at **G** rather than having a head-on smash a split-second later. That would depend on how close **B** was and what evasive action he was taking if any.

Going too fast like this into a corner is *pure bad anticipation*. U must get your act together and avoid it!

The back of your car can swing round on you as quick-as-a-flash purely as a result of ignorant, uncontrolled, excessively hard braking.

Ultimately, any car braked too hard will go like this into a spin, though this is unusual unless the braking is continuously excessive and starting from high speed.

If the back of your car ever *does begin* to come round under extreme braking you have to react to it very fast. You need to do more than just straighten the steering. *You must steer into the skid*. That means steer the same way as the back is sliding: left if the back skids left, right if it goes towards your right. Immediately that skid subsides you need the steering straight again as you continue battling to brake without "locking" the wheels any more.

If you are too late and you go round never give up! Try to stop before you run backwards into something. Equally, be ready to reverse further, out of people's way; or, if you are now going forwards again, to steer out of danger.

When you see an amateur ahead panic-braking, be ready for that potential spin . . . Get your own speed in sufficient control to stop or steer clear. On dual carriageways and motorways, multiple pile-ups are not uncommonly started by such a braker braking too hard and getting into an *unnecessary* spin. His car wallops into those closest by and the incident soon escalates as others, *driving too close anyway*, follow suit . . . This is one reason why you need such long, long gaps at high speeds on our over-crowded trunk roads.

In **PART TWO** I mentioned how anti-lock brakes, if your car is fitted with them, solve the whole wheel "locking" problem. In effect they do the unlocking for you. They have another life-preserving advantage. Because your wheels won't lock you never lose your steering.

You can be steering for safety *during maximum braking*, where others will be struggling to free off slithering front wheels before they can do so.

Even with anti-lock brakes you would be foolish to brake fiercely and swerve all at once unless you had no choice. Nevertheless they are a powerful tool and, if you have these brakes, you should get some emergency stop practice where you can deliberately add a little steering. Then you can appreciate "live" what this extra steerability means.

OVER-ACCELERATION SKIDS

Chart fig. 80 defines these.

This exercise will give you first-hand experience of the wheelspin of an over-acceleration skid. With an experienced teacher (who may like to demonstrate first) find a gravelled drive where you can obtain permission and there is no danger, and where you can sweep the stones back afterwards. Alternatives might be a rain-soaked empty car park or an already muddy edge to a playing field, again, with permission!

Do a standing start in 1st using fierce acceleration as you let the clutch fully up quite sharply. The driving wheels should spin at first. You stop that at once by cutting your acceleration. *Don't touch your clutch pedal.* There is no need. The skidding ends almost the moment you cut your accelerator and you immediately regain control of the steering if it was lost. Likewise, loss of any sideways control at the driving wheels will be scotched. You can drive on calmly (almost) as if nothing had happened. However, if room is restricted, remember to stop!

This type of skid can occur as easily when accelerating from one speed to a higher speed (e.g. 12 m.p.h. to 25 m.p.h. in 2nd gear) as it can on starting from rest. It is most serious at high speed where it can result from harsh acceleration while cornering. If you are crazy enough to over-accelerate *downhill* the consequences are likely to be made worse . . .

Prevention

(a) <u>avoiding mechanical defects</u>

Keep your car mechanically safe. Pay special attention to the potential defects shown on chart fig. 80.

(b) <u>watching road causes</u>

The best prevention is anticipation. So watch for skiddy surfaces. Be extra gentle when accelerating on any of the suspect surface materials in chart fig. 80.

OVER-ACCELERATION SKIDS

One or both driving wheels spin rather than grip the road. (Once *one* of a pair of driving wheels spins, taking most of the power, the other will be much less effective at moving the car. This is why in the extreme slipperiness of snow you often see a car stuck, with one wheel spinning, but no forwards or backwards progress being made.) There may be loss of sideways control at the driven wheels end of the car as well.

Note: Most small cars have front wheel drive. Some, mainly bigger, cars have rear wheel drive. A growing number have permanent four wheel drive which is excellent. It seems practically to eliminate the problem of wheelspin skids of this type! A few cars have electronic sensoring to match power at each wheel to the available grip. This too minimises the wheelspin.

CONTRIBUTORY CAUSES

(a) mechanical defect
Soft or over-inflated tyre(s), slow punctures.
Bald driving wheel tyre.
Overloading or unbalanced load.

(b) road cause
Wet surface.
Slippery surface (oil, etc.).
White lines (wet).
Loose surfaces (gravel, sticky wet leaves, mud etc.).
Cobbles (wet).
"Black" (invisible) ice/"freezing rain", ice/snow.

(c) human error
Ferocious or jerky acceleration, especially in the lower gears, is the main cause.
The above when steering round a corner or bend makes a skid more likely.
Using too low a gear on ice etc.

Not allowing for (a) and/or (b) type causes is the chief culprit leading to these skids.

Fig. 80   Over-acceleration skids.

202

Expect wheelspin, even with minimal acceleration, on anything as nasty as snow or ice. The wheelspin that happens so easily on that needs to be minimized by, at all times, using the *highest* gear that will still, without stalling, manage to move the car off, or keep it going if you are already on the move. On the level, start off in 3rd or even in top.

The secret of climbing hills on snow is to select the appropriate highest gear (see above) at the bottom and try not to change it going up. Another secret is to select fresh snow where you can. This will give you better grip than beaten down snow. However, in your eagerness to take to untrodden snow, mind that the camber of the road, running into the gutter, doesn't cause you to slide right into the edge. If you watch how others ahead of you are getting on and keep yourself spaced out (from them!), you may be able to avoid stops, or pick less slippery parts for them, and thus avoid getting stuck.

In snow or mud, if you do stick and a driving wheel just spins, stop it immediately. Usually the more spinning you allow the worse it gets. Try reversing off the skiddy patch with very low revs, or even "rocking" forward and backwards alternately, again at very low revs, to see if you can climb away from it. If people are prepared to push, let them try while you are in *neutral*; then spinning your wheels won't defeat their objective – or spatter their faces! If anything apart from a tow, or digging out, is going to work, that will.

(c) eliminating human error

Never accelerate harshly. You should have discovered in the experiment above how this applies to moving off. But remember not to be too punchy picking up speed after turning a corner into a new road, or as you drive on out of a bend on the open road.

On ice or snow such mistakes can have dramatic consequences. These skids, particularly if you have rear-wheel drive, can develop too quickly to catch and correct them before damage is done. Once you've experienced the tail of a rear-wheel drive car snaking out on ice, you will know what I mean!

On wet roads over-acceleration skids present an almost sneakier risk because one wet surface can be very much more slippery than another. Take no chances.

Correction

Important as it is to cut your acceleration instantaneously, *you mustn't do so completely.* Only reduce it sufficiently and for long enough to kill the wheelspin.

To stop all acceleration if a skid happens when going fast on a bend, may turn a skid of this kind, usually correctable, into a skid of the next (*sideslip*) type, from which you may well not be able to extricate yourself. Whilst adjusting your acceleration (which is often all the cutting of it need amount to) correct the steering as necessary. Directly that wheelspin subsides gently re-accelerate. This sets your car back on course.

You should thereby regain control. As you continue on your way *think*: was it caused by over-acceleration or the road surface? If it was mainly the latter *slacken speed to a safe level* or you will soon be in another skid, possibly a more serious one.

Dramatic tail-end breakaway such as I referred to above (with rear-wheel drive) should never happen unless you are exceptionally clumsy with your accelerator. However if the back does snake right round so that your car is on its way into a spin, you must steer into that skid pronto – in much the same way as suggested for a braking-induced spin earlier. That instant reaction must go hand-in-hand with cutting your acceleration to stop the wheelspin that is making your back wheels slide.

If you are quick enough to win control, you must straighten up fast, and resume *light* acceleration at once to set you back on course as just stated.

SIDESLIP SKIDS

First see chart fig. 81 which describes these.

They are too deadly to suggest any exercise to give you experience. I urge you to assimilate these notes, anticipate, and avoid such serious skids.

Prevention

(a) avoiding mechanical defects

Don't overload and do look after your car. Give special attention to tyres, brakes, and suspension. Any faults are often first noticed through peculiarities in your steering. So, if the steering itself checks out OK, investigate anything odd in those other areas too.

(b) watching road causes

Make generous allowances wherever you know surfaces are skiddy or doubtful. For examples, check over the road

THE DEADLY SIDESLIP SKID

All the wheels, while still rolling forward, drift, skidding or sliding off their steered course. *The car is almost completely uncontrolled.* Sometimes called 4-wheel drifting, the condition is considerably more deadly if the rear wheels are slipping away quicker than the fronts. Very often a front (or steering) wheel skid is the precursor of a 4-wheel drift, though it can happen on its own, in which case it is marginally more controllable. The effect and the measures to be taken are in general the same. *Sideslip* skids usually only happen as a result of a car being cornered too fast or after excessively hard braking, perhaps, though not necessarily, on a bend.

CONTRIBUTORY CAUSES

(a) mechanical defect
Bald tyre(s), slow punctures, soft *or* over-inflated tyre(s).
Overloading, unbalanced load.
Poor springs or faulty shock absorbers (these lessen the up-and-down reaction of a spring after a bump).
Front (or back) wheels not having tyres of matched tread pattern, *condition* or type.
Faulty brakes.

(b) road cause
Wet surface.
Slippery surface (oil, etc.).
White lines (wet).
Wind.
Flood water.
Loose surfaces (sticky leaves, gravel, mud etc.).
"Black" (invisible) ice/"freezing rain"-ice/snow.
Adverse camber.
Bend.
Downhill.

(c) human error
Cornering too fast for conditions is the prime cause.
Excessive speed can be the cause (even going straight) if *aquaplaning* becomes involved.
Not making allowances for (a) and/or (b) is the fundamental fault that lands drivers in these dire skids.

Fig. 81 *Sideslip* skids.

causes in chart fig. 81.

Adverse camber, come upon too jolly fast at a bend, can set the scene for a *sideslip* skid, and redouble its severity if it happens. Multiply that again by some "steepness factor" if you are going downhill . . .

Wind normally only seriously affects a car travelling above 50 m.p.h. or so. Whereas in a gale high-sided vehicles may get turned on their sides, an exceptional gust in a high wind is more likely to blow your car – sliding – several metres across the road. The effect is most dramatic on wet roads. Watch for gusting wind whenever you emerge past a windbreak such as a bridge or a belt of trees. Be prepared too, every time you pass a big lorry. Hold the wheel firmly to guard against violent wind from wherever the source . . .

Flash-floods can leave undrained surface water sheeted across the road for many minutes. Country roads where drainage is poor are very prone to the problem. Hitting this sort of sheet of water can produce *instant* deadly *aquaplaning* – even at below typical aquaplaning speeds, for which see on. Make sure you are gripping your steering firmly. Hitting one on *only one side of the car* can so violently unbalance you as well, that the car is set off into a spin. Your reaction in such a spin would need to be razor-sharp along the same lines suggested on pages 200, 204 and 209.

Aquaplaning **DOESN'T REQUIRE SHEETED WATER TO HAPPEN.** It will occur on any wet road if you drive too fast.

Aquaplaning describes the phenomenon in which on a wet surface tyre-to-road grip gradually lessens as speed rises until the front wheels, instead of gripping, stop turning and scull on a microfilm of water that builds up between them and the road. Just as a water-skier skims over the surface at speed but when he stops sinks, so front wheels can "ski" and "sink" – with grip only returning when they sink and roll again.

In *all* types of car this front wheels aquaplaning effect is likely to begin on an ordinary wet road around 65–70 m.p.h. Cars built for speed are not immune . . . drivers of such expensive machinery please note. (This critical speed will be reduced where road drainage is poor. And it will be severely reduced on a bald or balding tyre. This is because a tyre depends upon its tread pattern in order to displace water out behind itself.)

Above the critical speed *your car is out of control*.

You have NO STEERING. Your front tyres are out of

touch with the road. With luck you may hold a straight course. But you have had it if you need to turn . . . And the slightest wind gust or change to the precarious overall balance of your aquaplaning car can throw you at the mercy of the gods. If you sink back to the road unevenly, that too can shoot you off in practically any direction you like to name.

Prevent such terrible dangers by keeping speed on wet roads *below* 65–70 m.p.h. I have seen several cars spin off straight roads and motorways, their drivers, presumably, unaware of what aquaplaning can do.

Excessive speed in other slippery conditions can also lead to the almost total loss of control of a *sideslip* skid. The most ferocious of these is probably black (unseen) ice, where that loss can be so unexpected. At least on snow and most other obviously dodgy surfaces, you should already have speed right down and ought to have been expecting trouble.

(c) <u>eliminating human error</u>

Constantly weigh up changing road surface factors. Accept any minor braking or over-acceleration skid as a **MAJOR WARNING**. Ignore them at your peril. At corners, always use the "Slow in *drive* out" technique to minimize *sideslip* risk.

I can promise you that, if you habitually corner too fast for conditions, especially downhill ones, the day will come when the ugly trio I talked of earlier – centrifugal force, momentum and adverse camber – will combine to slam you off the road in short order, with plenty of slither but no dither . . . The car will appear to slide bodily off the far side of the corner because the initial steering force applied will have first turned it partly sideways.

More often than not it will be your front wheels that actually give first (a front-wheel skid) but the rears will probably join in so fast as makes no difference, turning the skid into what amounts to a 4-wheel drift.

The reason why the front wheels are normally the first to slide is that your car has what is known as *understeer* built in. The overall balance of the car is designed to uphold this characteristic because it is safer than its opposite number *oversteer*. An oversteering car would break away at the rear wheels first. That has been proven to be a much less stable state of affairs because rear-end breakaway at high speed tends to be uncontrollably instantaneous.

A front-wheel skid, on the other hand, has some hope of redemption, as does a 4-wheel drift where the rear wheels break away only *after* the front ones.

Never upset the balance of your car by jerky steering during cornering. Close to the limit of adhesion that could trigger a skid the moment the grip of the front tyres is upset. Make your steering habit reasonably gentle and progressive. Adding on small steering movements little by little as you progress round a long and tightening bend will help you retain the feel of how well your car is balanced; in contrast, over-sharp movements that then have to be corrected back are asking for trouble.

Correction

Sideslip skids can happen as easily in a tight corner at 50 m.p.h. on a wet road as at 5 m.p.h. on iced-over snow. Very often you crash or leave the road before you have had much chance to think. They happen suddenly and develop even quicker.

You may be able to stop excessive-speed *aquaplaning* (see page 206) before it turns into a *sideslip* front-wheel skid or a 4-wheel drift off the road, or even a spin, if you have room simply to ease off your accelerator till your wheels hit the deck and roll again. You don't want to brake and "land" in a locked-wheel aquaplaning skid such as was described earlier on page 191. (That could occur – or continue – down to a much lower speed.) Nor would you want to "land" with your steering wheels on the turn . . .

You are more likely to survive after aquaplaning on a sheet of flash-flood water – which makes it obvious – than when you are doing it from sheer excess speed on a wet road – where you probably won't realise what is happening until too late. In a front-wheel drive car you *might* get an advance warning if the front wheels suddenly started to wheelspin at 65 + m.p.h. But be warned, you don't get any such clue with rear-wheel drive or with 4-wheel drive.

Unless, happily, you come out of *aquaplaning* unscathed, you are likely to find the exit is straight into a front-wheel skid or a 4-wheel drift.

These *sideslip* skids, as I have called them – more usually triggered by idiotic speed at corners – all need tackling along the same lines.

If there is room and time you must steer into the skid much as you would in trying to prevent going into a spin under too-heavy braking or in over-acceleration wheelspin rear-end breakaway. See page 200 and page 204.

In *sideslip* you have to steer like lightning towards where the *front* is disappearing. Once/if the rear goes you may have to steer further into the skid to try to counteract that too. You have to be just as quick, or quicker, to straighten up, the instant steering control comes back; otherwise you will go where you have steered, which is what you are trying not to do!

You must hope that you win this steering battle and that your *sideslip* skid will be absorbed both whilst you neither brake nor violently decelerate – and that that will happen in time to steer for safety.

You have to hold a touch on the accelerator in order to propel the car (hopefully) towards where you want it to go. Nil acceleration, or worse, braking, merely plays into the hands of that ugly trio above.

However it is no good correcting a *sideslip* skid – any more than any other skid – if that effort takes you directly into a head-on smash. The decision to abort, as on page 200, may have to apply here too.

GENERAL ADVICE ON SKIDS

NEVER DRIVE AT A SPEED FROM WHICH YOU CANNOT STOP **WITHOUT SKIDDING,** IN THE PRE-VAILING ROAD CONDITIONS, WITHIN THE DIS-TANCE YOU CAN SEE IS CLEAR. Think what this means at blind bends and brows of hills . . .

Round the next blind corner a Learner, exiting to the right from a private driveway, could have stalled with his car straddled across the road!

My final words on skids refer again to adverse camber. When you overtake you are often exposed on the "wrong" camber. You must allow, should any emergency crop up, that that could cause a crucial problem for you. If you suddenly had to pull back it could mean a skid where otherwise there might have been none. As you can't allow for it when it is too late, you have to consider it *before* – during your overtaking planning. That could mean, for example, cancelling an over-take on a wet day that might have been safe in the dry. If you were going downhill too, you would probably cancel it anyway!

When you see a fool cornering too fast towards you, watch the camber. Will it push him on into you if he skids? A correct forecast can save your life if you are able to drive accordingly to keep out of his way.

At lefthand bends keep well in to take advantage of the

camber. In an unpredictable slide, for example on black ice, an extra metre or so and a bit of helpful camber can be your saviour. Lacking that metre and gripped by adverse camber immediately, can spell your doom. In fig. 79 if U had been closer to your edge you might, despite your late braking, still have escaped the trouble I described.

On righthanders, however, you should never cut corners. Slow up more.

Experienced fast drivers extend similar principles to roundabouts and to wherever they can keep camber working for them, rather than against them. On roundabouts, for example, they hug the roundabout edge on the way round (when traffic permits) and then "skim" the lefthand pavement as they enter their exit road. They know the value of keeping the camber to their advantage and of always gaining the maximum safety margin against skids.

MOTORWAYS

Learners are not allowed on motorways. On Test you may be asked a few M questions. At the end of the Question and Answer section which follows this you will find some example ones, many of them designed also to expand your practical motorway skills.

GOING ONTO MOTORWAYS

When you are going to make a long motorway journey first confirm you will not run out of fuel. Re-fuelling service areas can be relatively few and far between. When you drive fast you burn fuel quicker so keep an eye on the gauge. If ever the next fuel stop is signed as probably being too far ahead, turn off; never risk running out.

Slightly higher tyre pressures are usually recommended for motorway speeds. So before you go, look into that in the "book of words" supplied with your car.

Engine oil and coolant levels ought to be checked weekly or at least once in every 1000 miles. Make sure it has been done. Motorway speeds quickly test the "weak points"; overheating or seizure, which could happen if levels were low, is *very* expensive. Watch your oil pressure gauge if you have one.

Filthy spray ejected behind large vehicles on motorways during inclement weather can blank out your windscreen in a second or two. You must know that you have a *full* windscreen washer ready to cope. A weekly top up should keep you right, remembering in winter to add an ice-inhibitor, *which is then essential*, but be warned that you may be unable to drive safely without being able to clean your screen.

As you join the motorway you merge with left-lane traffic. The procedure is exactly as outlined for **Turns** *Onto* **A Dual Carriagway** in **PART THREE** page 153, except that the scale is normally much bigger; you have a much longer acceleration slip road to help you merge on smoothly; you usually need to accelerate with much greater whoomph to match your speed to that of left-lane traffic before you can merge safely into a sufficient gap within it.

Watch from a motorway bridge one day. You will see how the snags related in **PART THREE** as above can unfold.

You should also note how quite a few smarter left-lane drivers move out of that lane if they are able to, before reaching any point where new traffic comes in. See also **Do Unto Others . . .** a little later in **PART THREE**. Otherwise, if you are travelling along in the left lane as people are merging out, it is best to try to keep a steady speed. That helps the joining driver(s) to make correct decisions. However, you still need to keep an eye on every joiner who might not have seen you, or who may make a genuine misjudgment. If there is one who clearly hasn't prepared himself for stopping at the end, you may need to slow down quickly so that he can get out in front of you before he runs out of acceleration slip road! Alternatively, you may realise that by speeding up – quite early on – you can thereby help a joiner by making it 100% clear to him that he will need to come in somewhere behind you.

One more snag particularly seems to affect joining a motorway. It is the possibility of a motorway middle-lane driver – to whom you would have to GIVE WAY – returning to the lefthand lane at the very same moment that you are about to merge out into it. The most likely time to be caught out is when you are poised to nip out ahead of a steady stream coming along, perhaps one which is headed by a lorry in front of which you know you have ample acceleration to forge ahead. Because of the narrow sight lines which you have, that lorry can easily conceal that middle lane driver till too late. too late.

This is one reason that I have stated that mirrors are not enough for these merges. You need a physical look across your shoulder to spot such a snag before it is too late for you to hold off making your merge.

LOOKING FAR ENOUGH AHEAD *AND* BEHIND

I am convinced that the principal cause of motorway accidents is failure to look – and focus – far enough in front.

Lift your eyes to the horizon.

Is traffic up in front *there*, moving? Is it moving well all the way betwixt you and there? If the steady flow has changed in any way you should be on the alert *already* slowing down. If it is bunching anywhere between you and that horizon, *fall back*. If those immediately ahead of you are closing up together, or braking, take the red alert (from their brake lights) seriously.

Double or treble your distance behind them NOW. Nothing is easier than catching up again. Except being caught out, unable to brake or stop quickly enough. That's deadly easy.

Keep your distance (behind other drivers) just as emphasized in **The Gap To Leave** in **PART TWO.** I hope you will re-read that section now.

From a vision point of view you must have *as well*, a longer gap when behind a lorry than if following a car. On a straight motorway, where those next in front of you can themselves block your view ahead of them, you also need longer following distances than on a curved one where the curves allow you to see past the vehicles immediately ahead.

Of course, you must keep an eye on the man you are first behind; he may run out of fuel, or half swallow a wasp, or have any crisis resulting in plunging about unexpectedly. Yes, you must be watching individually the next dozen or so vehicles ahead of him spread out between all the lanes.

But, *above all*, comes watching *that flow*, or lack of it, that is running 30 or 60 vehicles ahead, or however many vehicles there are to be counted way out up in front as far as the eye can see.

At 70 m.p.h. it is the drivers who correctly foresee trouble *up there*, who survive, and help everyone round them survive too. At night, and in heavy rain and spray, they are the ones who make our motorways continue to be as safe per passenger mile as they are. Whether you drive that fast or not, join them.

A prerequisite of looking far enough **BEHIND**, before changing lane in either direction, is looking **FOR LONG**

ENOUGH. Only my **Mirrors, Mirrors, Mirrors** drivestyle of early on in **PART TWO** can suffice.

Before moving out to overtake remember some drivers exceed the national speed limit by a hefty margin. They are up on you in no time. Give extra moments accurately to assess someone's speed relative to yours, before deciding to go before he catches you up. A nifty glance out of the corner of your right eye over your shoulder, should prevent being caught unawares by a driver already committed to passing you, but hidden from your mirror because he is already too close – or perhaps because he has already been skulking there for some time.

Such drivers "sit" outside and behind you for considerable distances with, apparently, no intention of passing. They are wrong to do so. They should move in behind you, or pass. (However, to be fair, they may have for some while been blocked from completing the latter by people ahead of themselves.) If you are sure that sitting there for no good reason is what someone is up to and that his speed is the same as yours, and you wish to overtake whatever is *ahead of you*, you have to "merge" carefully out ahead of the miscreant in much the same way as you merge onto a motorway to begin with. Make sure you signal ample warning and that there is plenty of room.

Before ever moving in, remember that criminal motorway drivers don't stop at breaking speed limits; they try to nip past you on your left too . . .

MOTORWAY RULES

Essentially there is no difference between the rules for motorways and those for all other multi-lane dual carriageway roads. I set them out early in **PART TWO** under **Dual Carriageways**, under **Lane Discipline** also in **PART TWO**, and in **Dual Carriageway Overtaking** which is the last section in that **PART**.

Do please refresh your memory of those sections before your first drive on any motorway. Do it that same day! Many of the tips in them apply with re-doubled force on motorways. Because of the high speeds you must stretch the forward planning of your every move even further ahead of that you would use on ordinary roads.

SLOWING, STOPPING AND LEAVING MOTORWAYS

On motorways even long-experienced drivers can lose all

appreciation of speed; 70 m.p.h. feels like 30 m.p.h. If you are overtired you can even imagine, having dropped to 20 m.p.h. from 70 m.p.h., that you are now going backwards!

What amounts to hallucination in the latter case is clearly very dangerous.

STOP DRIVING IF YOU ARE EXHAUSTED. Tiredness kills.

Never drive fast hour after hour on a long motorway run.

Take 10 minute breaks and walk around at a service area at least every two hours.

If you feel drowsy before you can leave a motorway, slow down and move into the lefthand lane if you are not already in it. Then try opening your windows, singing, whistling, wriggling in your seat etc. but don't let these affect your driving. If you still can't shake off sleep leave the motorway at the next available point, stop and allow yourself forty winks to recover.

After many miles at high speed it is all too easy to fail to slow early enough for your exit turn off, or for when you see a traffic block ahead, or when you reach the end of the motorway. It is always worth *double-checking on your speedometer* as you slow up that you are indeed getting down to an appropriate speed. This can save you from an awful scare moments later.

When you can see ahead that your lane is stopping, flash your brake lights to give early warning to all behind. If it is a sudden stop – especially just after a curve and where the stopped traffic is yet hidden from those behind – add your 4-way hazard warning lamps until your mirrors confirm that everyone behind is *OK for stopping* too. (See also **Warning People Behind** in **PART TWO**.) Aim to pull up with a few car lengths in hand. You can always choose to use some of them up, if the first to arrive from behind you clearly won't be able to stop in time. However, in the event of a "concertina" smash from further behind, at least you may avoid hitting whoever is in front of you, as well as yourself being biffed from the back. Once the position behind is safe, close up the gap you had left in front of you.

QUESTIONS

On Test you will be asked questions based on the Highway Code. Some of the questions that follow are of the kind examiners ask. You will soon discover from them how well you *really* know your Highway Code. Others introduce important driving techniques not touched upon elsewhere in this book.

QUESTIONS (Answers begin on page 217.)

1. Can you cross double white lines unbroken on your side?

2. When must you *not* sound your horn?

3. Is there a national overall speed limit for cars?

4. If someone wanted to overtake you when you were doing 40 m.p.h. in a 40 m.p.h. limit, would you try to prevent him?

5. What do twin flashing red lights and gongs denote?

6. How should you approach a Pelican Crossing?

7. What is meant by a U-turn and is it legal?

8. What must you do after driving through flood water?

9. In a built-up area how do you determine the speed limit if there are no signs to be seen?

10. How should you treat a cycle lane?

11. Must you stop when a policeman signals you to do so?

12. What does the law make you watch for before getting out of a car?

13. To which side of the road should horsemen keep?

14. What is a yellow "box" junction? What rules apply to them?

15. If you fail to stop at a **STOP** sign will you be failed?

16. Why are correctly inflated tyres essential?

17. If the driver in front signals or his brakelights come on, what do you do?

18. Where is it unwise to park?

19. If a pedestrian or motorist waves you on, would you go?

20. Which sign denotes no overtaking?

21. Which sign means priority over approaching vehicles?

22. How should you park at night?

23. What are the shortest stopping distances, for good conditions, given in the Highway Code from 70 m.p.h., 60 m.p.h., 30 m.p.h.?

24. What is the routine given in the Highway Code that should be followed for every manoeuvre?

25. When in a traffic queue, what should you remember when you come to a zebra?

26. How should you park between two cars at the kerb?

27. Describe: (a) the "contra-flow bus lane" and (b) the

"bus lane on road at junction ahead" signs.

28. What does a single broken centre line along a single-carriageway road mean if the markings are long and the gaps are brief?

29. At traffic lights do you go once amber comes on to shine with the red?

30. What special action and considerations should you take when reversing?

31. Never drive nose-to-tail over one; never drive onto one unless you can see that the road is clear on the other side; never stop on **OR IMMEDIATELY BEYOND** one, are all Highway Code warnings about what?

32. What by law must you do when parking?

33. What view will the examiner have about driver-courtesy?

34. Signs which give ORDERS are mostly of what shape?

35. What is the usual shape of WARNING signs?

36. What First Aid advice does the Highway Code give?

37. What must drivers know about buses and bus lanes?

38. What rules affect loads carried?

39. What extra care must you use going in or coming out of property adjacent to a road?

40. If you wanted to park for a very few moments in a potentially obstructive position, would you switch on your hazard warning lamps?

41. "If you are involved in an accident which causes damage or injury to any other person, or other vehicle, or any animal (horse, cattle, ass, mule, sheep, pig, goat or dog) not in your vehicle, *or roadside property*" what *by law* must you do? And what else should you do?

42. If anything falls off your car which could be a danger to others should you stop to pick it up?

43. What legal requirements govern the condition of your car's tyres?

44. Why must you never stop at the roadside as shown in fig. 89?

45. A red **X** or a white downward-pointing arrow are sometimes lit up on a gantry above different lanes on a multi-lane carriageway. What do they mean?

46. Where should your current car tax disc be displayed?

47. How would you turn to go back the other way on a busy major road – too busy to contemplate a U-turn or a three-point-turn?

48. Is the Highway Code law?

49. Describe the clearway sign and what it means.

50. A series of low black and white banded posts each with a red reflective patch at the top would be found on which side of the road to tell you what?

51. An apparently straight and flat road can sometimes conceal fast traffic coming towards you. How?

52. What does a slow lorries sign look like?

53. If you bash a kerb at speed (10 + m.p.h.) but your tyres *seem* all right, what should you do?

54. How does the stick of a deaf *and* blind person differ from the usual white cane of a blind person?

Motorway Questions (Answers from page 229.)

1. Does the Highway Code allow reversing on motorways?

2. How should you treat fog on a motorway?

3. If you miss your turn-off what should you do?

4. On a motorway can you overtake on the left?

5. Is there a minimum motorway speed limit?

6. Do you ever *have to stop* on a motorway?

7. What do flashing amber signs behind the hard shoulder on some motorways mean?

8. If travelling fast on a 3-lane motorway, would you drive in lane 1, 2 or 3 (numbering from the left)?

9. At the first sign of roadworks what should you do?

10. What sort of temporary signs can you expect to see on motorway flashing-amber-and-lit-panel signs?

11. If you need to stop on a motorway where should you do so? What counts as "need to stop"?

12. If you are in the outside lane on a motorway, overtaking other traffic, and a car appears behind with its right indicator flashing away, what would you interpret this to mean?

ANSWERS (For *Motorway Answers* turn to page 229.)

1. No, never, except to avoid an accident or obstruction.

2. At night (after 11.30 p.m. or before 7 a.m.) in built-up areas, or if stationary (unless to avoid being hit).

3. Yes, it is 70 m.p.h. on dual carriageways and motorways, and 60 m.p.h. on all other roads.

4. No; you are not a policeman. He may be a doctor, etc.

5. A level crossing with a train due. You STOP! The train cannot. You are likely to die if there is an accident. Study your Highway Code extra carefully on this. You must know exactly what it says about all types of level crossings. See

page 187 regarding breakdowns on them.

6. Here in sequence are the rules for drivers:

1. Green	**GO.** (Use normal care. Pedestrians should wait. But don't trust them; watch them too.)
2. Continuous amber	**STOP** (unless unsafe to do so).
3. Red (high-pitched pulsating tone may tell the blind they can safely cross.)	**STOP!** (Walkers have right of way; **N.B.** *you still have to stop and wait for 4 below, even if there are none, or if those there are have crossed already.*)
4. Flashing on-off amber	**GIVE WAY** to pedestrians still crossing (but you should go if the crossing is clear or if any pedestrians are comfortably clear before green comes on again).

7. See fig. 82. Legal except where signs ban it and – naturally – in one-way streets. Position close to kerb. When traffic is clear *in both directions* swing into full lock to get round and away in one. Leave time for a three-point-turn lest you misjudge the width. Sometimes U's are helpful if you need to turn to go back the other way on a dual carriageway. Approach the next junction which has a good-sized *SAFE AREA* **for turners** (see page 151) exactly as if you were going to turn right. Check for the absence of any "no U-turn" signs. At the appropriate moment, if the U is going to be safe from every point of view, as well as legal, convert your "right turn" into a full U, going into the left lane of the other half of the dual. This can sometimes be done safely at a traffic light if you have enough time to get right round on green. However, wherever you intend to do it, always allow plenty of extra time for its completion, and for the fact that other people may not immediately spot what you are up to.

8. Try out your brakes. They can lose *all* power. Drive slowly, gently holding the brakes on with the left foot till efficiency returns. *Do this at walking speed*. Less than 25 metres should be enough to sweep/drain/steam the water off your brake linings.

9. Wherever there are street lamps you *assume* a 30 m.p.h.

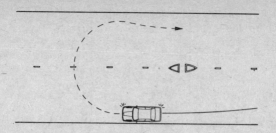

Fig. 82   A U-turn

limit is in force. If any different limit applies you will see
"repeater" signs attached to lamp or other posts.

10. Keep off! Neither drive in nor park on one. Look in
your Highway Code for a minor exception to this. Before
crossing a cycle lane **GIVE WAY** (naturally!) to bikes. Note
that bus lanes are frequently cycle lanes too; look out for
riders whizzing alongside the buses.

11. Yes, with care. The safety of doing so is your
responsibility.

12. That opening the door is safe; watch behind for cars,
cyclists and motorcyclists – *look over your shoulder*. Remind
passengers. Teach children that they should get out on the
pavement side – *and* – that they should look out for
pedestrians before they open the door.

13. Horse riders keep left but beware! Sometimes the
horse takes charge.

14. Any junction having criss-cross yellow lines painted
thereon. The principle involved is that, if your exit off a
major route junction is blocked, you shouldn't move onto it
yet; then you can't easily yourself become a blockage to
someone else.

The rules are demonstrated by fig. 83. Imagine a queue of
traffic ahead of lorry **B**. **U**, intending to go straight ahead,
wait this side of the yellow criss-cross box as shown, even
when the light is green, if traffic in or beyond the box has
built up and blocked your exit from it. Don't go until you see
at least area **C** is clear. But you can move up during green,
ready to turn, if you are going to be turning right and only
await a gap in oncoming traffic through which to do so.
However, if drivers from opposite you will also be turning

219

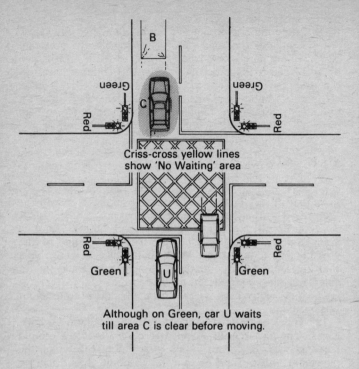

**Criss-cross yellow lines
show 'No Waiting' area**

**Although on Green, car U waits
till area C is clear before moving.**

Fig. 83 A "Box" junction.

right, be reminded of fig. 60 and the commonsense approach that is needed, before any silly rushing forward.

15. Yes, for breaking the law.

16. Because it is a legal requirement. Because of the increased dangers of skidding (see chart figs. 78, 80, 81 and text there). Under-inflation also causes the tyre walls to flex too much. The excessive heat and wear which arises may lead to a side-wall burst. The tread will wear rapidly at the outside shoulders. Apart from the skidding danger, over-inflation additionally causes a bumpier ride and quick wear to the centre of the tread.

17. Act. Be guided by his signal – your examiner is noting whether you react quickly enough by raising your foot off the accelerator at once, and then preparing to slow down or

change lanes or whatever, if necessary.

18. Study the comprehensive list in your Highway Code. Always pull off the road onto a parking area if you can. Never wait or park where your car could obscure a traffic sign or an on-the-road mark, or otherwise become a hazard – especially the indirect one of blocking someone's view. There are quite a number of places where even stopping to drop off or collect passengers is banned. I'll leave you to work them out from your Code. If only we were all less selfish and enforced our own personal ban on dangerous places to stop there would be a great many fewer fatalities on our roads.

19. At your own risk! *Do not rely* on others' judgment.

20. A red circle with a white background inside on which two equal-sized cars appear, the lefthand one in black, the righthand one in red.

21. A blue square with a thin white border; a large white arrow on the left side points up, and a red arrow (smaller) on the right, points down.

22. If you cannot answer this with ease after Question 18 above then you have a lot more work to do on your Highway Code. Search the Code text and the law extracts at the back for specific rules about having to leave lights on when you park at night.

23. 70 m.p.h. – 96m, 60 m.p.h. – 73m, 30 m.p.h. – 23m.

24. "Mirrors – signal – Manoeuvre."

25. To leave the crossing itself clear. Do not queue on it.

26. You should always face in the same direction as traffic on your side of the road. Figs. 84–88 show the stages in sequence. Unless a space is a clear 3 car lengths longer than your car, it never pays to try and go in forwards. So here I deal with shorter spaces which are, of course, the problem ones. Judging if a short space is long enough will come with experience. 1½ metres longer than your car is probably a minimum. Judgment of the whole manoeuvre is greatly assisted if you do some trials on an open space first, using the cardboard boxes and tape of **PART ONE**. (Hitting parked cars is costly!)

Signalling left with your indicator, stop beyond the space, parallel to and with the back of your car slightly ahead of the back of the vehicle next forward of the space. Aim to pull up for your "Start Position" with slightly less than a full door's opening width between your car and the other car. (A slow glide to a stop just beyond the space, together with your indicator, should be enough to make your intentions clear to

Fig. 84 Kerbside parking between cars: start position.

Fig. 85 Kerbside parking between cars: stage two – full lefthand lock to get you in.

Fig. 86 Kerbside parking between cars: stage three – lock change-over to (full) righthand lock.

Fig. 87 Kerbside parking between cars: stage four – a little further to go on full righthand lock before you are "in", ready to straighten up.

Fig. 88 Kerbside parking between cars: final stage – leave your car in the middle of the available space.

anyone behind. Hopefully they will stop short to leave you room. However, for first attempts, choose a road and a space at a time when little other traffic is likely. You don't want any initial inexpertise to hold up queues of people in a hurry! I assume for the purposes of the rest of this explanation, that your, by now, innate safety-conscience will cause you to make all necessary checks for danger to other traffic – e.g. from your front wing swinging wide as you progress – and for idiotic pedestrians marching across the very space you are backing into.)

Reverse into the space taking almost immediate full lefthand lock to get you in. Very slowly does it for this "Stage Two". The nearside back corner of your car should head for the kerb at the mid-point of the length of the space.

Before the back *wheels* are within ¾ of a metre of that kerb, and as soon as you think your front wing will clear the car in front you change back to the other lock (fully). During this lock changeover of "Stage Three", car speed must be so slow as to be barely observable. Only that miniscule pace will give you the chance to be certain that you won't biff your near side front wing.

For "Stage Four", that wing now clear, stay (or get) on full righthand lock so as to bring the car fully round, parallel to the kerb and "in". Once parallel to the kerb, speed still being hardly discernible to the onlooker, use any more backing space available to straighten up.

"Stage Five" – still straightening up if required – is a matter of making sure you leave the car in the middle of the space. Then, if either the car ahead or the car behind needs room to manoeuvre, it is there for them.

One or two "shunts" back and forth may be regarded as normal to make sure you leave your car tucked in correctly within 1–2 tyre widths of the kerb. If it ever looks as if you will need to "shuffle" more than that, the chances are that you would be better to pull right out and start again fresh.

27. (a) Rectangular, with a blue background and a thin black border; a picture of a bus and a direction arrow are reversed out in white on one half of the panel, and these are separated by a vertical white line from the other half, which has a white arrow (inside a thin white rectangular border) showing the direction of normal traffic flow.

(b) Rectangular, black border, white background, picture of bus, plus flow-direction arrow and the words "Bus lane", all in black.

28. Hazard; unless you can see well ahead don't cross that line!

29. No. This amber light only alerts you that green is coming. Nor should you go ahead at green until there is room for you to clear the crossing (see Question 14 above).

30. Find someone to guide you if you cannot see clearly; watch for children, motor bikes etc. *immediately* behind the car; if in doubt get out and look; GIVE WAY to all comers; never reverse as far as a centimetre further than is essential; never reverse from a side road into a main road.

31. Railway level crossings. If you didn't get this right return to Question 5 till you *really* know about them. If you did cross and stopped "immediately beyond" a level crossing, anyone who had moved on to the crossing behind you would be stranded there, probably facing death or terrible injury. That he may be foolish is hardly the point; we can all look after him by never crossing until there are **TWO** or more vehicle spaces the other side. One day it could be you who made that absent-minded mistake.

It is a good idea to approach main-line level crossings in low gear even when you don't expect to stop. Use 3rd or 2nd as appropriate. Then, if there are suddenly signs of a train when it is *genuinely* too late to try to stop, you are geared to speed up and get through safely.

32. You must switch off the engine and set the handbrake. At night you must dowse headlights but leave on sidelights where the law so requires. You must obey all general waiting restrictions as well as any specific ones for that place. (You may not park on a pavement except in rare places where local signs ask you to do so.) See also **Hill Parking** at the end of **PART ONE** and Question 22. Apart from on a one-way street the nearside of your car should always be next to the kerb. You should lock your car and also attend to the other aspects of security in your Highway Code.

33. He will expect to see it at all times. For example, if someone wants to overtake you on a single-carriageway road, you may be able to help him by slowing down and moving in a little at an appropriate moment.

34. Circular – but two vital exceptions are the octagonal STOP sign and the triangular GIVE WAY sign.

35. Triangular but a few are rectangular.

36. Check the Code and learn this minimum knowledge thoroughly.

37. In towns you should always GIVE WAY to a bus

which is ready to move out from any bus stop if it's safe for you to do so. You should watch for passengers walking out from behind stopped buses – or jumping off moving ones!

Outside their period of operation which is always sign-posted *all drivers* can use bus lanes (other than contra-flow ones). **DO** do so and help unblock the unnecessary jams these lanes cause. You are warned that it is illegal to "dive" into a bus lane just to pass someone ahead of you who is waiting to turn right. You may not park in a bus lane during the hours it is operational unless to load or unload.

38. They must be secure, must not project unsafely or be likely to endanger yourself or others, and you must not overload.

39. Check pavements first: GIVE WAY to pedestrians. Pavements are for people – not motor vehicles.

40. Don't park there! These lamps should only be used to warn others of a *genuine* obstruction, for example, when you have broken down.

41. *No matter how slight the accident you must* **STOP**.

First calmly organise – if you are still able-bodied or can delegate to someone practical and quick-witted – to prevent further carnage from fire, or from more traffic running into the crashed vehicle(s). Hazard warning lights on, engine(s) off, NO SMOKING, help being called, First Aid begun, children and animals rounded up to a safe place, are the major priorities. Warn people not to stand where they obscure hazard warning lights from traffic coming either way.

It is wise to carry a Highway Code permanently in your car so that its accidents section and First Aid advice are to hand to remind you of everything else to think about.

The law's demands about obtaining and giving information are all reprinted in it too, so that you can follow them through properly once everything else is under control.

As well as a Highway Code you may wish to carry your insurance certificate and MOT certificate (if applicable). The police or others may need to see them and it can save problems if you have them at the time. However, do keep these documents well hidden in your car. They might make it easier for a car thief to sell it! Police will only accept sight of the original documents, not photocopies.

Make sure you get the other driver(s) name(s), address(es) and insurance details, plus the registration numbers of all vehicles involved. If any pedestrians are hurt you need their names and addresses too. Get addresses of any friendly witnesses if you can as a legal case might turn on their evidence. Sketch at the time what happened and take measurements. It is worth taking photos if you have a camera.

Do not admit blame. That may be a condition of your insurance. Fault may not be yours or wholly yours anyway.

42. On ordinary roads yes, but be damn careful. Have someone stop traffic first if need be. On motorways no; it is too risky altogether. The Highway Code tells you to call the motorway police from a roadside telephone.

43. Your tyres must all be suitable for the vehicle and the use you are making of it, e.g. heavy-duty tyres may be required when a vehicle carries loads. You have to maintain the correct air pressures, and can be in default of the law if any tyre is worn to less than 1mm depth of tread. This requirement is expected to be put up to at least 2mm soon. More than the legally demanded depth of tread must show, over at least ¾ of the tyre width all round. So bald patches are outlawed. No bulges or cuts in either of the side-walls are allowed; nor are cuts across the tread area of more than 10% of the tyre's width permitted, if they are deep enough to affect the body cords. (Any cord *showing* anywhere makes a tyre illegal to use.)

Wrong combinations of radial and cross-ply tyres are illegal. The front wheels must *both* have tyres of the same type which *must not be radials* unless *all four* wheels have radials. The back wheels may have a pair of radials while a pair of cross-ply ones are on the front. But I strongly advise against this. It is best to stick to all radial or all cross-ply tyres. Then you can arrange for the front wheels, where well over 75% of braking grip takes place, always to have the best pair of tyres, evenly matched for wear. The rear pair of tyres ought also to be evenly worn.

Tyre law is re-examined by Parliament quite frequently. Reputable tyre suppliers can keep you up to date on current regulations and can explain the differences between types of tyre.

You should be aware that, if you knowingly drive with a defective tyre, the cover on your insurance policy may become void, or effectively void, in the way I mentioned in my **GENERAL GUIDANCE** at the beginning of this book.

44. Because such stopping is illegal. It unnecessarily forces anyone passing you to have to cross the double white line. It would be illegal to stop on the *other* side of the road here too.

No stopping is allowed on either side where there are double white lines of any sort.

Fig. 89 Where **NOT** to wait or park!

45. A red **X** facing you above a lane means that that lane is *closed* to you. (Oncoming traffic may appear along it at any moment!) You must change to a lane open to you – one designated by a downward-pointing white arrow – at once, or stop if need be before you can do that.

46. The legally correct position is at the bottom left corner of your front windscreen.

47. Ideally, turn left down a minor road, then find a side turning off that to reverse into before making your way back to the major road to turn right. *Never*, as your Highway Code warns, reverse from a small road to a bigger one. If you decide to reverse directly off the major road, have a good squint down the side road as you pass it to start with, to see

that it's suitable and empty of traffic.

48. No but courts are unlikely to allow rule-breaking to go unpunished.

49. A circle having a red border and a blue background with a red **X** across it. It denotes a piece of road, usually of several miles in length, where you may not stop except in emergency or breakdown or because of a queue. You may not stop to load or unload unless a qualifying plate below the sign allows this; nor are you allowed to drop people off or pick up passengers.

50. On the left where a country road narrows or bends. White patched markers will often be seen on the righthand side too.

51. When it dips down-and-up between you and the horizon. Dips deep enough to hide traffic are deadly. Not only can they turn an overtake into a nightmare; they can turn a (hidden) horse and cart into a death trap, if motorists speed recklessly.

52. A lorry climbs a steep gradient, all in black against a white background, within a red triangle border. Take notice – you fast drivers – that, especially on motorways where the incline is less obvious, left and middle lane drivers will soon be wanting to pull out ahead of you so as to pass the juggernauts.

53. Have an expert check them over as soon as possible and have your steering checked out for proper alignment. (If that has been upset your tyres would wear rapidly.)

54. It has two reflective red bands.

Motorway Answers

1. No. It says you must not reverse or turn in the road, or cross the central crash barrier, or drive against the traffic.

2. With the same caution as elsewhere. See the beginning of this **PART FOUR**. Your Highway Code devotes a large section to fog. Study that too. An extra problem in fog on a motorway is the lack of any pavements or nearby buildings or whatever, both to get your bearings by and to sense your actual speed. Lane markings or edge markings may be all you have.

The coloured stud scheme used to define the edges of motorways at night is a great help in fog after dark. The studs show up in your headlamps. Therefore you should know which edge you are near . . . and where acceleration or deceleration slip roads end or begin, etc. Make sure you understand which colours are used where, both from your Highway Code and from making a point of noticing what these studs actually look like on a clear night sometime.

3. Keep going to the next exit slip road.

4. Never, ever! Unless you are in a queue and traffic is also queuing outside you. See also page 76. All the rules apply equally to motorways.

5. No but it is unwise to go below about 40 m.p.h., even in the nearside lane, because of the high general speeds on motorways.

6. Yes, if traffic in front of you has pulled up; in emergency to prevent an accident; if required to by police, emergency traffic signs, or for a flashing red light above your lane if you are unable to move to an open lane.

7. Danger – you must drop to 30 m.p.h. or less when the lights are flashing, until you are sure it is safe.

8. If empty 1, if it is full 2, and for passing only 3. There is, however, no need to duck in-and-out between every lane 1 vehicle if you are going quite a lot faster than them. You can treat the lane as full unless the distance between the vehicles is considerable, and, if you were to go back to lane 1 between each one of them, you wouldn't just be moving out again straightaway.

9. *Slow up*: double-check mirrors and speedometer – prepare for single-lane conditions. Observe signs, signals and speed limits temporarily advised. Move lane if necessary. Contra-flow lanes, in force where traffic has to be shifted to the opposite carriageway, are the site of a disproportionate number of motorway accidents, despite strict enforcement of the speed limits. I'll say no more!

10. Temporary speed limit; lane(s) closure(s); change lane; leave motorway shortly; end of restrictions.

11. Nowhere, except in the circumstances of Question 6 above, or on the hard shoulder if you are severely ill or your car breaks down. (You cannot just pull onto a hard shoulder to consult your map. For all non-emergency stopping you must park at a service area or leave the motorway altogether; so – no stopping on entry or exit slip roads either!)

12. That its driver – very politely – is asking you to pull over as soon as possible so that he can pass.

YOUR TEST

A few weeks before your Test have your teacher run a mock

test with you. He needs a score card on which he can √ or ×
whether you are up to standard on the main skills examiners
watch for, as well as on the specific manoeuvres they put you
through. These are listed below with spaces alongside for
marking, should he prefer simply to use this book.

The extra weeks you have left will give time to polish up
items on which you are not yet up to scratch.

EYESIGHT TEST ; ENGINE START ROUTINE ;
MOVING OFF ; EMERGENCY STOP ; COURTESY
AND CONSIDERATION FOR OTHERS ; THREE-
POINT-TURN ; REVERSING INTO NARROW OPEN-
ING ; HILL START ; EFFICIENT ATTENTION TO
MIRRORS ; USING BRAKES/HANDBRAKE ;
STEERING WHEEL TECHNIQUE ; ACCELERATOR
CONTROL ; CLUTCH CONTROL ; CHOICE OF
AND SELECTION OF GEARS ; STOPPING SAFELY
AT KERB ; OTHER-TRAFFIC AWARENESS ; PAS-
SING PARKED VEHICLES ; POSITIONING ; SIG-
NALS ; USE EYES AT JUNCTIONS ; GIVING WAY
AS PER RULES OF ROAD ; ALLOWING PEDES-
TRIANS SAFE PASSAGE ; KEEPING TO SAFE
SPEEDS ; OBEY SIGNALS FROM AUTHORISED
PEOPLE ; KEEPING BELOW SPEED LIMITS ;
TRAFFIC SIGNS AWARENESS ; KEEP UP WITH
TRAFFIC ; MAKE DECISIONS REASONABLY
QUICKLY ; HIGHWAY CODE QUESTIONS AND
ANSWERS .

ON THE DAY

Your Test lasts up to about ¾ of an hour. It may seem long
but don't worry; the examiner needs to see how you cope in a
good cross-section of different traffic situations as and when
they arise.

His instructions will be clear. Any reticence to chatter will
not mean he doesn't like you; gossip could put some
candidates off their driving. That would be unfair. So don't
expect him to say much more than should be enough to put
you at ease and to conduct the Test.

Obviously your car must be in tip-top tune and generally
roadworthy. There must be no malfunction of the brakes,
steering, or major controls. The handbrake should hold the
car on the steepest hill. The tyres should have been examined
for condition and their pressures checked. You are also

231

legally required (i.e. not just for your Test!) to keep all windows *clean*, and to ensure that windscreen wipers and washers, horn, speedometer and *all* your lights are in working order. Your examiner can stop your Test if he finds that anything is wrong. Remember the law requires you to wear your safety belt. Fill up with petrol.

Be certain how long it will take you to reach the Test centre. You want to have 5 – 10 minutes in hand. Running late won't help your nerves! You can always amuse yourself, if you have to wait for long after you arrive, by giving some Highway Code items a final run through. Don't worry, however, if, when doing so, you seem to have last-minute forgetfulness. You are unlikely to fail for slipping up a little bit on one or two questions.

If you arrive quite early do announce the fact that you are there to whoever is in charge; there may have been a cancellation enabling you to go straight away.

Proof of identity is required. Take with you your (signed in ink) provisional driving licence (or foreign licence), or your passport, or an ID card issued by your employer. Also take your glasses (or contact lenses) if needed, insurance certificate, and MOT certificate if applicable, and your appointment notice all to the Test centre with you. Make sure your "L" plates are firmly in place.

If there is thick fog or ice, or snow, your Test may be postponed. Phone the Test centre and confirm.

Are you dressed warmly? We react better when warm. Remember your window may be best kept open ready for an arm slowing down signal. If the Test is in the morning I advise you not to go to it on an empty stomach after no breakfast. That can only encourage "nerves".

You should drive to the Test centre. This gives on the day confidence even if on the way, things go a little wrong; not to do so will certainly destroy that confidence.

You need not worry about exam nerves. The examiner has suffered from them before! He is well trained to note the difference between bad nerves and bad driving, and he won't penalize ordinary "butterflies".

AUTHOR'S MESSAGE

If you need advice with any aspect of learning to drive not explained here in this book, or you have any ideas which might improve future editions, I welcome your letters. Write to me care of the publisher and I will do my best to help.

Please enclose a stamped addressed envelope.

GOOD LUCK AND DRIVE JUST AS CAREFULLY AFTER YOU PASS – ALWAYS. And, by the way, remember to sign your full licence in ink when it arrives. That's the law!

INDEX

Also for learner drivers

CAR DRIVING IN TWO WEEKS

Over 1¼ million copies have been sold since this book was first written. Now in its 29th edition, it has been completely revised and updated to match the ever-changing conditions of our roads.

The Daily Telegraph: "Immensely practical".
Birmingham Evening Post: "Certainly the best".
Edinburgh Evening News: "A notable contribution".

TEACH YOUR SON OR DAUGHTER TO DRIVE

A book for learner and teacher to use together. It consists of ten lessons centred around in-depth analysis of the Highway Code. It sorts out what to teach, in what order and *how*. Amateur and professional instructors alike will welcome the way David Hough illustrates the correct teaching principles that most quickly develop a pupil's competence.

HIGHWAY CODE QUESTIONS & ANSWERS

To pass your Test you *must* know the Highway Code thoroughly and be able to answer the specific questions on it which your examiner will ask. John Humphries' book contains 300 questions and answers designed to make learning the Code an easier task.

Uniform with this book

For car owners everywhere

What To Watch Out for When
BUYING A USED CAR

Thousands of people buy second-hand cars each year. Sadly, many of them end up with vehicles which cost hundreds of pounds in repair bills. Make sure you're not one of them. Find out how to judge a car's merits, detect its faults and value it accurately.

Whether you're buying from a private individual, from a car dealer or at auction, this book will save you money!

EMERGENCY CAR REPAIRS

Are you helpless when your car breaks down or won't start? If so, Martin Davies can help. He shows how you can do something *constructive* instead of having to wait helplessly for the breakdown service.

No mechanical knowledge is required of the reader. The book shows where to look, what to do – even how to open the bonnet! Each investigative section is structured to get you rolling in the minimum time.

From the humble puncture to the mystifying ignition fault, this is the perfect standby that can save you £££'s.

Uniform with this book

OUR PUBLISHING POLICY

HOW WE CHOOSE

Our policy is to consider every deserving manuscript and we can give special editorial help where an author is an authority on his subject but an inexperienced writer. We are rigorously selective in the choice of books we publish. We set the highest standards of editorial quality and accuracy. This means that a *Paperfront* is easy to understand and delightful to read. Where illustrations are necessary to convey points of detail, these are drawn up by a subject specialist artist from our panel.

HOW WE KEEP PRICES LOW

We aim for the big seller. This enables us to order enormous print runs and achieve the lowest price for you. Unfortunately, this means that you will not find in the *Paperfront* list any titles on obscure subjects of minority interest only. These could not be printed in large enough quantities to be sold for the low price at which we offer this series.

We sell almost all our *Paperfronts* at the same unit price. This saves a lot of fiddling about in our clerical departments and helps us to give you world-beating value. Under this system, the longer titles are offered at a price which we believe to be unmatched by any publisher in the world.

OUR DISTRIBUTION SYSTEM

Because of the competitive price, and the rapid turnover, *Paperfronts* are possibly the most profitable line a bookseller can handle. They are stocked by the best bookshops all over the world. It may be that your bookseller has run out of stock of a particular title. If so, he can order more from us at any time—we have a fine reputation for "same day" despatch, and we supply any order, however small (even a single copy), to any bookseller who has an account with us. We prefer you to buy from your bookseller, as this reminds him of the strong underlying public demand for *Paperfronts*. Members of the public who live in remote places, or who are housebound, or whose local bookseller is unco-operative, can order direct from us by post.

FREE

If you would like an up-to-date list of all Paperfront titles currently available, send a stamped self-addressed envelope to
ELLIOT RIGHT WAY BOOKS, BRIGHTON RD.,
LOWER KINGSWOOD, SURREY, U.K.